A
Seed
THAT
Grew

MATHEW BENTHIN

WestBow
PRESS®
A DIVISION OF THOMAS NELSON
& ZONDERVAN

Scripture quotations marked NIV are taken from the Holy Bible, New International Version®. NIV®. Copyright © 1973, 1978, 1984 by International Bible Society. Used by permission of Zondervan. All rights reserved.

WestBow Press books may be ordered through booksellers or by contacting:

WestBow Press
A Division of Thomas Nelson & Zondervan
1663 Liberty Drive
Bloomington, IN 47403
www.westbowpress.com
844-714-3454

ISBN: 978-1-5127-6544-1 (sc)
ISBN: 978-1-5127-6543-4 (e)

Library of Congress Control Number: 2016919522

Print information available on the last page.

WestBow Press rev. date: 09/11/2019

Table of Contents

Seeds Are for Growing

For thousands of years truth has been subject to its generation,
The flame and shadows in Plato's cave in unending acclimation.
For thousands of years seeds of truth have grown into many fruitful trees,
Sons and daughters dispensing their father's love in glory or on their knees.
For thousands of years poetry has immortalized truth in a graceful rhythm.
Psalms and proverbs that ebb and flow with both freedom and wisdom.

These are the seeds that found their way to the soil of my heart,
Some by revelation and others by life's lessons that tear me apart.

"Reviving wisdom literature one stanza at a time."

-Mat Benthin

God's Sent Word

Your word went out and creation obeyed;
Your word went out and mankind delayed.

You take a fallen tree and build a temple.
You take a fallen temple and build a kingdom.
You take a fallen kingdom and build a world.
You take a fallen world and trade your sons for it.

Your way is beautiful in its day;
Showing us that sorrow is not here to stay.
Your favor more effective than all our labor;
Showing us that trouble isn't our only neighbor.

You are the light of life that satisfies.
One glimpse shares the fire in your eyes.
One whisper scatters your enemies like flies.
One touch and our selfish nature dies.

You call things into being;
We postpone faith till seeing.
Even eternity conforms to your every word;
We are lucky to keep pace with your advancing herd.
Your word goes out and creation has obeyed.
Your word goes out and your people are dismayed.

The Truth of a Wish

Be careful what you wish for, because you might get what you want but nothing more.
Mistake appetizers for the main course, and you'll
miss out on what eternity has in store.

For where your treasure is, there your heart will also be.
Even if it's shortsighted, your father can't ignore his child's earnest plea.
We live in a world that plants inferior wishes every day, so guard your heart.
For the heart is the wellspring of life, and all murky waters from there will start.

You end up getting what you want in this life and the next.
But a warped heart that gets what it desires remains unfixed.

Whether it be riches and recognition, or just a beautiful trophy wife.
A good father will always be asking what his child wants most in life.

We are all born into a world that is designed to inspire or satisfy dreams.
The best dreams grow bigger the more they are realized, or so it seems.
But some dreams are sent with us and end up as ash on the pyres,
While others spread across the land like unpredictable forest fires.

So fan the flame of desire when dreams are a wishful hope out of sight.
Do not let desire be satiated when you are rewarded with a little bite.

That Which You Have

A man can only receive that which has been given him from heaven above.
So if your convoluted efforts succeed examine your heart and deepen your love.
But when pure hope shatters, each shining piece be careful not to get rid of.

A man can only steward that which has been entrusted to hone his skill.
So if you harvest enough for a lifetime don't adopt a lazy and faithless will.
But when it's time to cut your losses, prepare to climb the next looming hill.

A man can only value and prize that which was set into his weary hands.
So if masses follow your every move be sure to lead them to fertile lands.
But when a flock refuses to budge, surely death will meet it where it stands.

Less is More

The less you suppress your own heart and mind,
the more self-control you will be able to find.
But the longer you insist on running from a past mistake,
the more control it'll have and the more hope it'll take.

The less you venture toward greener grass on the other side,
the more free you will be within pleasant pastures to abide.
The less you daydream of an easier and better future,
the more diligent you will be to make your hopes secure.
The more you try to trail-blaze your own path,
the more you'll follow others toward certain wrath.

Emmanuel

It may be that Emmanuel means God is with us or among us;
The day marks an end to the times when our creator was distant.
It may be your birthday but on it you gave yourself as a gift to us;
The day you left your throne to be born as a helpless infant.
It may be your birthday but on it the king made a murderous fuss;
The day long desired when you would bring promises to fulfillment.
It may be your birthday but now it's a day of merrymaking for us.
The day your promised son from Heaven for sinners was sent.
It may be your birthday but you left home to build a home within us.

Only an fool would create a story of God born outside an inn with no room to stay.
Only a God who loves us as children would come himself to break our sinful fate.
Only and fool would manufacture a story of a child King worshiped in a bed of hay.
Only a God who wanted to bring all people into his family would dare incarnate.
Only an fool would lie about a virgin birthing the
Lord who birthed the world in a day.
Only a God who desired all men to ascend to Heaven
would descend to reveal life's gate.

Every year my birthday becomes less important and memorable,
While the value of your birth becomes more and more favorable.
Every year my birthday reminds me of bodily death that is inevitable,
While the love it took for you to come to us remains immeasurable.
Every year my birthday marks another year on a world that's miserable,
While the light of your life guiding me home becomes more comfortable.

Christmas is the day you came so you could guide as one just like us,
The night Emmanuel's star led the wise to a humble manger.
Christmas is the day your son came to live and suffer the same as us,
The night your love manifest faced cold and perilous danger.
Christmas is the day my best friend and savior came to free all of us,
The night your throne invaded Earth proved you aren't a stranger.

You Meet Me

You meet me in a dry and thirsty land;
With water for my soul in your hand.
You meet me in a dark lonely place;
With delight and a smile on your face.
You meet me in a garden half burned;
With favor I never could have earned.

The Paradoxical Heart

The hardest thing to do in life is to keep your heart alive.
Forsaking the crutches and pet causes that men contrive.

The easiest thing to do in life is to let your heart shrivel and die;
Forsaking the wounds that bring us to our knees before the lord on high.

The most uncomfortable thing to do in life is to obey every word he utter;
Forsaking the winds and waves that blow so long as he steer the rudder.

The most stunting thing to do in life is to take charge of your own growth;
Forsaking as trivial the planting and watering from Spirit and brothers both.

Like tilling away at soil whilst others are planting upon it;
An open eye reserved for the big picture your daily bit.
Like pulling at weeds scattered among wheat before harvest;
An open will sure to join in the handiwork of an impartial artist.
Like cutting out an organ along with a cancerous tumor;
An open pocketbook creates an heir out of a consumer.
Like refusing to have a joint set that was recently dislocated;
An open hand that both gives and receives from the anointed.
Like throwing a baby out along with its bath water;
An open schedule the best way to spin in the hands of the potter.
Like looking a gift horse in the mouth with a dentist's scope;
An open cup catches more of heaven's dew for popper of pope.
Like a child missing out on dessert by not eating the main course;
An open dam produces more than any stream cut off from the source.
Like sawing away at a dry branch whilst sitting upon it;
An open heart for your fellow man keeping you from the muddy pit.

To allow sorrow its rightful place amidst tragedies that sting;
That joy might bloom from the tear-watered soil we bring.

To allow hate its rightful place amidst injustices that repulse;
That love might outlast disgust which makes our stomach convulse.

To allow anxiety its rightful place amidst storms that never let up;
That peace might taste all the sweeter as we drink from his cup.

Hate is the key to love's door;
Held open for those who face their own hypocrisy.

Sorrow is the key to joy's door;
Held open for those who face toward living theocracy.

Foolishness is the key to wisdom's door;
Held open for those who face against cancerous democracy.

Death is the key to life's door;
Held open for those who face new birth into heaven's clerisy.

Avoiding pain is sure to cost you love;
Whose absence set to motion powers that compete and shove.
Avoiding stress is sure to cost you peace;
Whose absence narrows your vision to many a broken piece.
Avoiding death is sure to cost you life;
Whose absence foretells perpetual strife.

Repentance

My kind of repentance likes to turn from wickedness with words,
but even while I face toward his light I can still walk backwards.
Your kind of repentance would soon gouge out my eyes and heart,
but even as a heartless blind man I can share your glories in part.

He Declares

He declares, "Apart from me you have no good thing."
I wonder if a time will come when those words don't cause my pride to sting.
He declares, "I am the alpha and the omega, the beginning and the end."
I wonder if there's any joy in a story when you know what's around the next bend.
He declares, "I am who I am."
I wonder how many nicknames you have like the lion and lamb.
He declares, "I will be with you, even to the end of the age."
I wonder if the freedom I exercise is still just another comforting cage.
He declares, " I have indeed seen the misery of my people and am concerned."
I wonder if there was ever a time you were not aware or at what point you 'learned'.
He declares, "I myself will come to rescue my people from their oppressors."
I wonder if your continual grace will spur us to surpass our predecessors.
He declares, "I did not come to bring peace but a
sword that turns child against parent."
I wonder if i continue the same direction undeterred I'll eventually become hell bent.
He declares, "I am the way, truth and life; no one
comes to father except through me."
I wonder why the whole world is forever trying to bypass your gate when it's free.
He declares, "I am the bread of life and the blood of the new covenant."
I wonder if there will truly come a day when no longer need to repent.

Problematic Unity

When a damaged boy finds a damaged girl,
Can both their hearts transform into a flawless peal?
When a gracious man finds a gracious woman,
Both fountains overflowing will leave no good work undone.

Although it is not good for man to be alone,
What good is a crutch before you are fully grown?
Although it is not best for woman apart to be set,
What good is a suitor that turns a maiden into to pet?

Surely if the blind lead the blind they will both fall;
Surely if the broken mend the broken they will forever crawl.
Surely if the lost guide the lost the way of life they'll never learn;
Surely if the shrewd learn from the shrewd every bridge will burn.

When your best friend who swore to never marry finds a mate,
Don't be surprised if your friendship they soon begin to hate.
When your siblings follow a passing skirt or tail,
Don't be surprised when toward chaos they sail.
When your daughter finds flattering lips and shoddy support,
Don't be surprised when she trades her own heart to court.

Any romance that separates friends is surely adolescent obsession;
The rudder named love will turn toward possessive oppression.
Any unity that sends a bride back to a negligent Uncle's house is surely broken;
The daydream that promised to fulfill your dream you will dread being spoken.

What Are Words but Wind?

What are our words but wind?
Yet one of your words leaves your image forever twinned.
Like man's breath short-lived since our father sinned.
Yet one of your breaths bound spirit to dust that only death can rind.

What are our words that they stir your heart?
It is your echo alone that makes our voice stand apart.
What are our hearts that they stir your word?
It is your heart alone that sets us free as a bird.

What are words but obsolete communication?
Missing the mark by their intended nature.
Like a photo of nature's serenity is a pale imitation.
Like circus darts rigged against the player.

Like a toddler fumbling to stand up on his own
Begins thinking himself like his father because he can pick up a phone.

Like a child bashing pots and pans
Begins to think herself a musician playing for her fans.

Like a dog whimpering from its cage
Begins to assume he and his master are on the same page.

Surely your thoughts are higher than ours;
Our speaking as presumptuous as Babel's towers.

Surely your ways are higher than ours;
Our seeking as endless as a sandglass telling hours.

It was you who gave us words in the garden.
We who disregard your words by tasting the forbidden.
It was you who traded your word for many a new son.
We who discarded your son who left sin's curse undone.

If one of our images is worth a thousand of our words,
What is one of your words worth?
Yet your precious word and image were the same from birth.
Undiminished glory portioned in thirds.

The pinnacle of our words is maturity.
The pitfall of our maturity is inevitable familiarity.
While your words betray our every security.

The pinnacle of our revelation is repentance.
The pitfall of our repentance is looking across the pasture fence.
While your word forever offers transcendence.

What words have never been spoken throughout the ages?
Even tomorrows prayers lay open like a familiar book's pages.

You say by our speech smudged or pure we will be judged.
You say the tongue is a rudder steering down streams worse of better.
But our loose lips are better at sinking ships,
And our sharp words cut others as easily as curds.
Our spontaneous worship as predictable as a salesman claiming entrepreneurship,
And our eloquent accolades like describing as blue your daily sky parades.

Surely it was not words but faith that made you marvel;
A soldier humbling himself before your authority.
Surely not words but unbelief that made you marvel;
Your hometown's men taking offense because of assumed familiarity.

The more our words the less the meaning.
The more your words the more the mystery.
The less our words the more wisdom will be speaking.
The less your words the more lavished our liberty.

Your word is living and active,
Fluttering through countless generations.
Our words are lifeless and at best destructive,
Falling idly across the nations.

To you, our words must pass bitterly like vinegar.
To us, our words linger like honey from choice nectar.
To you, our words must clutter like chaff without a breeze.
To us, our words can't be held at bay like any stifled sneeze.
To you, our words are sure to sound like lip service.
To us, our words are like choice cream rising to the surface.

Your raw word is unbearable;
Like a blazing fire before forests of stubble.
Your radiant word is contagious;
Like winter's flu, forever tenacious.
Your revered word is sharper than any blade;
Cutting flesh and soul like a barber clipping hairs frayed.
Your revealed word does not fade with time;
But haunts us longer than any rhyme.

To you, our words must pass bitterly like vinegar.
To us, our words linger like honey from choice nectar.

To you, our words must clutter like chaff without a breeze.
To us, our words can't be held at bay any more than a stifled sneeze.

To you, our words are sure to sound like lip service.
To us, our words are like choice cream rising to the surface.

As You Came, So You Should Stay

Though I came to you as a single man,
I still seek romance apart from your plan.
Though I go to you when the love among men grows cold,
I still offer your embers to the unworthy that I can hold.
Though I cherish your every word,
I still follow death's popular herd.

Though I came to your throne as a pauper and left as a son,
I still take detours back to the pigsty and leave your work undone.
Though I came to your court as a convict and left forever free,
I still set my cross aside to taste every fruit that seems good to me.
Though I come to your loving table weak and leave nourished,
I still starve myself of your presence until I become famished.

Surely I did not come to you with family in tow,
Yet I still seek a beauty with whom I can grow.
Surely I did not come to you with wealth and riches,
Yet I still hoard things every time the old self itches.

How am I to stay hopeless and friendless if I have your spirit?
Why do I forget your helping hand that holds my heart in it?
How am I to stay lost and alone if your words guide my path?
Why do I forget your children each need a daily bloodbath?
How am I to stay weak and weary if you are my daily bread?
Why do I forget your word regarding the only one I will wed?

When I came to your love I was an enemy to you and your ways,
Now you expect me to love my enemies to the end of my days.
When I came to your truth I was bound and broken by lies,
Now you expect me to set every heart free; that, for truth cries.

Why am I so skilled at wasting your grace and my own heart?
Surely you are the only one perfect in love, and we'll never part.
Why am I so occupied with scrounging out a place for myself among men?
Surely you are the only place my heart will ever belong outside my own skin.

Homecoming

Seated at the grandest of banquet halls,
A seat reserved for every daughter and son.
Greeted by a festive crowd within homely walls,
A greeting of ceaseless feasting and endless fun.

Though I was not seated near those I had held dear,
The joy laid before me could halt even the briefest tear.
With one glance I could spot many that had honed my will,
But many were absent that I had taught with truth and skill.

I recognized and knew many friends I have yet to meet in this life,
But I could not find the groom despite the celebrating of his wife.
The realization of our suspicion that heaven's kin know and are known.
The chosen family of strangers unified by the fruit of the seed sown.
Though many hearts I had loved deeply were seated far from me,
I've known all along it was never my love that sets others free.
Though I knew some were present because of my tearful prayers,

I have no credit to take from the one who paid all of our fares.
I was surrounded by brothers I had yet to teach or guide.
Though I knew them, I had yet to meet them on this side.

Even the lowliest seat would have been more than I deserved.
In just a moment the harvest of my entire life could be observed.
Surely a heart sinks when delusions of grandeur are cast aside,
Surely his kingdom grows with each fool that escapes from pride.

Surrounded by kingdom brothers and sisters in the truest sense.
There was one thing that had not changed despite providence.
Among those absent was the host of our blissful banquet;
Everything good and true laid before me and I wanted none of it.
Among the vacant seats was the head seat of our host and groom;
The only one whose words can make even the tiniest seed bloom.

This was the one thing that had not changed in the least part,
I must turn from many good things to seek and find his heart.

The Only One

Only one thing more powerful than the cords of sin;
Your third string of love that binds two as if of the same skin.

Only one thing more stubborn than our straight path in the wrong direction;
Your unjust love for prodigals that are prone to test their own election.

Only one thing more resilient than our cockroach-like desires;
Your kingdom seeds that spread like thorns and briers.

Only one thing runs deeper than the drought of our soul;
Your ocean of love that floods creation to make us whole.

Only one thing more scandalous than our adulterous backsliding;
Your grace too good to be true but calling wretches from their hiding.

Only one thing deeper than our self-inflicted wounds;
Your patient approval as your hopeful son prunes.

Only one things more fluid than our conformity to this world;
Your ambition that your spirit might be forever unfurled.

Only one thing more precious than our petty stories;
Your adoption that paupers might share in your glories.

Only one thing more comforting than the prisons we organize;
Your promises so grand they almost sound like lies.

Only one thing more tempting than our apathy;
Your offer to bear our wounds and burdens in sympathy.

Only one thing more binding than our curse;
Your persistence noted in your word's every verse.

Image to Nature

Let us make man in our image!
That creation might follow after the promised son's lineage,
And through the ages raise him to be mature.
That he might also share our divine nature.

Let me show you he is born of fallen man's root!
Soon many illegitimates tasting bittersweet fruit.
Let me show you it is darkness that he harbors in his heart!
Soon ground drank Abel's blood tainting creation from the start.

Let me show you his days will be cut short in his brothers' thresh!
From Adam's seed will come the spotless lamb from above.
Let me show you his hope will turn to dust along with his flesh!
From David's seed will come the exalted king to reign in love.

The firstborn among the dead returning with hordes at his back.
The firstborn in spirit and truth found worthy will nothing lack.
The chasm between man and maker forever mended.
The gates of hell rendered obsolete as he ascended.

Let me show you they are destined for amnesia and numbness!
Let us wean them with the milk of their elder brother's spirit.
Let me show you they will kill their own hearts for ignorance's bliss!
Let us witness the maker's nature bud and blossom from tainted grit.

Dream Reality

Only in my waking hours am I blind;
Blind to the goodness in your faded image;
Image whose unwritten fate we create as we grind;
Grind away at the harvest from our saintly lineage.

Only in my waking hours do I forget;
Forget the pleasure my heart to those with eyes to see;
See that even felt needs you satisfy leaving no room for regret;
Regret reserved for death as you willingly pay its costly fee.

Only in my waking hours do emotions eclipse faith;
Faith the lonely path never far from death's highway;
Highway whose frequent heart tolls turn a man into a wraith;
Wraith that puts its father Satan's will and image on display.

Only in my sleeping hours can my troubled spirit return;
Return to its home an eternity away, yet as near as my breath;
Breath whose sighs express more than any words I could learn;
Learn today that glories flicker and wane till made permanent by death.

Only in my sleeping hours can I clearly see;
See my place in your assembly divine.
Divine branches grafted into the loving trinity;
Trinity that demands fruit of its every vine.

Only in my sleeping hours do I remember;
Remember the pain our flawed love brings your heart;
Heart whose flesh makes us whole forever;
Forever the nonsensical goodness that sets us apart.

Suffering Servant Standard

I lavish love on others, despite staring into apathy's face every day.
Self-treating one's own heart ensures death's mark will forever stay.
I give hope to others, despite my own hopes being well out of sight.
Self-imposing one's wishful thinking on the world spreads strife's blight.
I offer wisdom to the swerving, despite my own seemingly aimless path.
Self-navigated routes all lead to one highway cluttered by children of wrath.
I mend the wounds of the bleeding, despite having bled out long ago.
Self-inflicted cuts and injuries that fester beneath the surface as we grow.
I give living water to the parched, despite having only tears to drink each night.
Self-fulfillment topping off your cistern by packing rocks and debris in tight.
I show mercy to those who wrong me, sparing them the blows that set me straight.
Self-contentedness repelling hearts whilst gravitating everything deserving of hate.
I include the shy and shunned, despite never reserving for myself a place.
Self-fulfilling prophecies invading hearts with each look into one's own face.
I feed nourishing words to the weary, despite staying hungry every waking hour.
Self-reliance adding walls and gates concealing a malnourished heart within a tower.

Too often forgotten by those I keep in my mind and prayers.
Content today to tap into how much my father cares.
Too often scorned by my kingdom family.
Content today to juggle divine affairs clumsily.
Too often overlooked by those who need me most.
Content today to see the ceaseless work of the holy ghost.
Too often rejected by the stiff-necked keepers of God's court.
Content today to join in my elder brother's favorite sport.
Too often murdered by the ones I spend my life on and for.
Content today to see life begins by walking through death's door.
Too often replaced by one who rules over the ones I cherish.

Content today to head homeward though my flesh may perish.
Too often replaced by the wolves among the flock.
Content today to stand firm and lofty on the rock.
Too often bitten in the helping hand I reach out.
Content today to navigate alone the narrow route.

Walking as an incarnation of wisdom weighty and dense,
But kneeling as a fool spouting folly and nonsense.
Walking as a dispenser of comfort,
But nursing wounds that still hurt.
Walking as a shepherd empowered by your breath,
But kneeling while my own herd nibbles me to death.
Walking as your suffering servant,
But kneeling as a dissipating currant.
Walking as a contagious light to the world,
But kneeling helpless as an infant curled.
Walking as an heir to God's glorious kingdom,
But kneeling a son of man balking at freedom.

Choosing to love deeply kin who skim the surface.
Meanwhile our hearts are purified as in a furnace.
Choosing to live a destitute life to be worthy of him.
Meanwhile forsaking home and family on a divine whim.
Choosing to comfort the ones who ignored our tears.
Meanwhile we remain silent as the shepherd sheers.
Choosing to pour into leaky earthen vessels.
Meanwhile Israel with his Lord forever wrestles.
Choosing to bear burdens not my own.
Meanwhile kingdom seeds are sown.
Choosing to give the love I'll never find.
Meanwhile down the hidden path I wind.

Choosing to be patient with ticking time bombs of emotion.
Meanwhile bearing my cross to keep homeward motion.
Choosing to be merciful to those who think they've done no wrong.
Meanwhile facing iniquity's price like a son of man before a lifeless throng.
Choosing to be gracious to those who think they've earned my favor.
Meanwhile even the blows from your rod and staff I will savor.
Choosing to be gentle to those who rub me the wrong way.
Meanwhile patience only comes when I retreat alone and pray.

The sponging of disease by ignoring temporary health.
The sponging of darkness by casting aside our wealth.
The sponging of death by taking low roads in stealth.

Looking on as strangers devour the fruit of my toil and labor;
Never tasting the harvest that comes from loving my neighbor.
Looking on as the bird I nursed flies into a poacher's trap;
Creatures of habit that only glance at life's road map.
Looking on as my noble hopes are bulldozed over;
As easily as a bully tears the leaves from a prized clover.
Looking on as the objects of my affection retreat from my wooing;
Wandering from green pastures like a foolish cow mooing.

Abandon hope all yee who descend Sinai's peak;
Truth's scroll uncontainable till his words you speak.
Abandon faith all yee children who seek heaven's one-way door;
Having seen the substance of your faith you need hope no more.
Abandon wealth all yee who seek enduring riches;
A farmer sowing, planting, then in joyful harvest pitches.
Abandon fertile lands yee who long to see his promises fulfilled;
Pilgrims in progress passing from glory to glory forever thrilled.

Allowing darkness to be darkness so the light of the world might shine;
The paradox that all which is yours you intend to be mine.
Allowing sin to be sin so the everlasting redeemer might redeem;
The paradox that our fallen world is less enduring than an inspired dream.
Allowing death to be death so the light of life might rise in our lives;
The paradox that even during seasons of drought your word thrives.

Your pierced heart the price to share it with me.
Though death take its toll in the end I walk away free.
Your broken body the price to piece me together.
Though my parts drift to earth's corners like a feather.
Your homelessness the price to point me homeward.
Though mystery still envelope your every guiding word.
Your isolation the price to reserve a place for me.
Though I forsake that too if there I don't find thee.

Spread the Word

When a thousand demons leave a single man,
spread the word that God's kingdom has began.
When a sinful woman is forgiven and showers love,
spread the word of our adoptive brother from above.
When the weak and weary find rest for their soul,
spread the word that his daily bread makes us whole.
When prodigals turn from pleasure and toward life,
spread the word that his truth can put an end to our strife.
When the lost are sought out and carried back to green pasture,
spread the word to the least of these that they have divine stature.

But when blind men see, don't shout the word at village square or tree.
But when dead children rise, don't whisper a word of death's demise.
But when lame legs walk, don't tell the crowds that love to gawk.
But when lepers are made clean, don't brag lest spiritual infants never wean.

Boys and Girls

The heart of every boy says, "Look what I can do!"
Identity stuck to actions for better or worse like glue.

The heart of every girl says, "Look at me and don't look away!"
Identity stuck to the value you place on them with what you say.

Men are to be doers of deeds that will spread and nourish Truth's seeds.
Creation's masterpiece charged with tilling Earth's and humanity's weeds.

Women are to bear pain in order to birth both grace and new life;
Creation's centerpiece bringing balance to the world's endless strife.

Communion

When hope has drifted out of sight,
And I'm left without a reason to rise; let alone fight.
Tossed this way and that by waves of doubt.
I will look behind and listen to the echo of his once strong shout.
When memory of him drifts beyond thought's reach,
And I'm left clinging to others' faith like a leech;
Extracted then quickly tossed aside to wither in the mud.
I will look behind and soak up yesterday's atoning blood.
When desire for this life is drowned in peace or sorrow,
And I'm left willingly blind to tomorrow.
Tossed by the wind; stuck between heaven and Earth like a kite.
I will look behind (to his words of life) and take today's bite.

Poured Out

Often will lips let loose a sound;
A trail of notes wonderfully wound.
But the mouth moves only air,
Regardless of how loud you make it blare.
There is a song from the heart.
Few choose to take part.
In the constant beat
of tears splashing at feet.
It wears us out,
But it is the only route
To the one whose attention we seek.
An iron gate keeps out all but the meek.
The password is a wordless song.
One kept at bay far too long.
If we do not shed our tears for him or her,
The helper's attention we will never stir.

Where Have I Been?

How many years do the wounded waste asking where you have gone?
All the while you call out for them to change what they fix their eyes upon.
How many tears have you shed at our side while we recoil from your touch?
All the while we call out not to be healed, but just for another reliable crutch.

If there is ever a day, hour, or moment where you are absent, I will forsake you.
But if there is a love that isn't afraid to live up to the challenge of my needy soul,
It will have earned my unwavering trust and it'll deserve my eternal affection too.
My words and deeds will speak of the only one that wouldn't hesitate to pay my tole.

In the middle of the night I listened to the long-forgotten songs of joy from my youth.
My heart stood at a fork in the road and refused to retrace the same muddy path.
In the middle of my life the joyful parts of my soul
found their way back to my inner booth.
I can't help but ponder where my truest self has
been these many years skirting wrath.

Despite countless regrets, I would not change anything
that has helped me know you better.
Though I would change nothing, if I could start afresh
with lessons learned I'd walk straighter.
But if I had walked more straight, I would not know
the depths of your love for each sinner.

There has never been a single day my father hid his face,
There has never been a single hour without his spirit of grace.
There has never been a single step where he; with me, lost pace.

Change

What is it that changes a man;
And alters destiny's short life span?

Is it awareness of self, world, and others?
Then why do I struggle to love even my brothers?
Is it crisis that matures us as our heart stretches?
Then why do I avoid the eyes of unfortunate wretches?
Is it education that betters and broadens the mind?
Then why does it narrow till I'm one of a kind?
Is it love that floods from the heart into all senses?
Then why are couples shriveling up behind fences?
Is it success and a growing list of God-approved accolades?
Then why are we so quick to cut down taller grass blades?
Is it when we finally reach the greener grass on the other side?
Then why does it get yellow and patchy the longer we abide?
Is it the birth of new life making an adult out of a spectator?
Then why does a small life soon smother that of its creator?
Is it beauty that pierces with awe inspiring sounds and sights?
Then why do I settle for what I see without conflict or fights?
Is it towering achievements that form the building blocks of the past?
Then why are so many content to hide in the long shadows they cast?

But if it's your heart and only your heart that changes a man,
Then why do we scamper to and fro neglecting your plan?
But if it's your blood and only your blood that changes our fate,
Then why do we seek to bypass your blood demanding gate?
But if it's your commission and only your commission
that broadens our narrow minds,
Then why are we content to spend our lives in offices hidden behind closed blinds?
But if it's your work and only your work that softens our heart's soil,

Then why does our rockiness always compel us to toil?
But if it's your word and only your word that overwrites our reality,
Then why do we worry others might see yesterday's duplicity?
But if it's your heart and only your heart that changes a man,
Then why do we worry as if we could extend our short lifespan?

To Bloom is to Wither

Two souls bumped into each other.
Need was brought to life in parting;

Knowing you wanted no other.
The romance of your life was starting.

Love has struck your heart.
Floating on clouds you will start,

But then your love turns tart,
And you hide your love deep down to be smart.

When your heart races,
And your hunger fades.

When tight are your heart's laces,
And feelings circle your head making air raids.

Now your life is a playground,
And heartache the biggest bully.

Now your life is below ground,
And heartache will grind you fully.

A season when heartache reigns;
Marking your life with fiery stains.

There are no battle wounds to show;
Only missing pieces to a heart that others can never know.

Intimate Branches

You are the heart of my heart,
And you are the love of my love.
That will not change though we part,
Stay as fierce as a hawk and as pure as a dove!

Before your light shined in my life,
All I could do was survive the world's strife.

But with the piercing of eyes,
And the tasting of your soul's waters;
This tree flourished and sprung up to the skies!
And from now on will drink from the dew of heaven.

But alas, it is time for you to spread your wings and fly.
So I won't weigh you down with countless heavy words.
Smile, scream, laugh, and never forget to cry.
For that is how we sift burdens like a baker his curds.

The world will try tell you who you are and what you ought to do,
But I say, "Be a blank slate till God reveal his intention for you ever true."

Agape

Love begins like the first tick of a time bomb;
A heart destined to shatter like that of a prodigal's mom.
With periodic explosions of emotion like birth pains;
Highs and lows making their lasting mark like blood stains.

Destined to shatter and scatter into shards of the soul;
Forever un-mended despite a lifetime of damage control.

True love only begins when we decide it will never end.
True love only vanishes with our sight of it beyond the next bend.
False love began when I wanted to make you mine.
False love dies when I trust your good is also mine.
True love began when I was charged with your care by the living vine.
True love wains only when we turn our backs on its source divine.
True love drew near us both when you were beyond my reach.
True love wains when beyond our substitute roles we breach.
True love's spell began when I heard your heart's song;
Flesh put to sleep and spirit awakened after so long.
Self-love's curse lifted as your burning heart singed my binds;
Unconditional love that only a child of grace ever finds.
Two jigsaw pieces jumbled then reassembled by their maker;
Intending to teach us to be a giver as much as a taker.

Love is only love if it comes from above.
Love is only love if it loves to love.
Love is not tested on a one-way highway.
Love is not tried by a flat tire along the way.
Love is not love if it expires or turns tart.

Love is only love if it grows, deepens, sweetens from its start.
Love is only love if it can't be returned or taken back.
Love is never love if you can purchase it like a toy on a rack.
Love is never stretched until pulled into eternity.
Love is never torn apart by outward enmity.

True love grows with desire to please its author rather than its object.
False love withers with submission that allows our pride to get wrecked.

Love is never love if it costs nothing.
Love is never love if it has conditions.
Love is only love if it shares new life like Spring,
Love is only love if its hand comforts like a physician's.

Surely your good is my good;
Any life, love, or joy poured into you soaks into my heart as well.
Surely your harm is my harm;
Any blood, sweat, or tears shed by you also drip from my heart's well.
Surely the muck from one muddies the other with its sin.
Any cleansing flow over one refreshes also its twin.

Past the Past

Who am I that my agenda endures though I am already dead?
I am your past that haunts you no matter where you lay your head.
Who am I that threatens to control who you are and what you do?
I am your past that digs up the skeletons you thought you outgrew.
Lay aside the comfort of bondage like a bum!
Absorbed in his or her story are those becoming scum.
Lay hold of truth and you will know its freedom!
Absorbed in the past are those presently numb.
Only a fool thinks he can outrun his past.
It is sure to follow him to the ends of the Earth.
Only the son of man's freedom holds fast.
It is sure to eclipse yesterday's deeds of fault or worth.

Where Have I Been?

How many years do the wounded waste asking where you have gone?
All the while you call out for them to change what they fix their eyes upon.
How many tears have you shed at our side while we recoil from your touch?
All the while we call out not to be healed, but just for another reliable crutch.

If there is ever a day, hour, or moment where you are absent, I will forsake you.
But if there is a love that isn't afraid to live up to the challenge of my needy soul,
It will have earned my unwavering trust and it'll deserve my eternal affection too.
My words and deeds will speak of the only one that wouldn't hesitate to pay my tole.

In the middle of the night I listened to the long-forgotten songs of joy from my youth.
My heart stood at a fork in the road and refused to retrace the same muddy path.
In the middle of my life the joyful parts of my soul
found their way back to my inner booth.
I can't help but ponder where my truest self has
been these many years skirting wrath.

Despite countless regrets, I would not change anything
that has helped me know you better.
Though I would change nothing, if I could start afresh
with lessons learned I'd walk straighter.
But if I had walked straighter, I would not know the
depths of your love for each sinner.

There has never been a single day my father hid his face,
There has never been a single hour without his spirit of grace.
There has never been a single step where he; with me, lost pace.

Forever Unknown

Forever unknown,
Despite many attempts to be shown.
Forever unheard,
Despite centuries of sharing your word.
Forever taken for granted;
Only for your benefits are you wanted.
Forever ignored,
So long as your gifts we can hoard.
Forever left out,
Until we set foot on your pilgrim route.
Forever unknown,
Though your willingness to shed blood or tears for us has been shown.

The closer you let us get,
The more of you will slip through our finger net.
The closer you come toward us,
The farther we shrink back; making a fuss.
The more you reveal yourself holy and pure,
The more we want to conceal our need for a cure.

Seeing your healing we forget your scars;
Scars that prove you love us more than all the heavens and stars.
Seeing your delight, we forget you anger;
Anger for how your house was less fit for you than a manger.
Seeing your joy we forget your sorrow;
Sorrow for Zion's chicks unwilling to follow.
Seeing your feast, we forget your hunger;
Hunger to do the father's will and reveal to brothers younger.
Seeing your fountain, we forget your thirst;

Thirst for us to drink of your mercy till we burst.
Seeing your light of life, we forget the darkness you sponge;
Sponge the filth our works could never manage to expunge.

How many friends did your miracles make?
Eyes demanded a sign to dispel their demise.
How many sheep the wolf try to take?
The paradox that only seeing you opens our eyes.
How many onlookers knew God's son had died at the quake?

Ears demanded the noise to dispel their fears.
The mystery that only hearing your voice opens our ears.
Mouths demanded the scraps to dispel their grumbling.
The mystery that your flesh through generations is still tumbling.
Eyes demanded the signs that prove a man spoke for God.
The mystery that the Lord incarnate be accused as a fraud.

The more you speak the more you prove us deaf.
Deaf to the one voice that can call us from death's clef.
The more you reveal the more you prove us blind.
Blind to the one whose face can renew our mind.
The more you guide the more you prove us fools.
Fools staggering this way and that to bend your rules.
The more you teach the more you prove us stupid.
Stupid to patch our bodies when it's our heart that's wounded.
The more you love on us the more you prove us selfish.
Selfish roots sinking deep even as our sin you banish.
The more you show your care the more you prove us apathetic.
Apathetic though any good standing we manufacture remains cosmetic.

How many thousands turned toward you for what you said and did.
How many thousands more turned away by what you did not and forbid.

From Maybe to Surely

Faith changes every maybe into a surely.
Surely our lives rest in your hands securely.

Faith changes every fancy that maybe this will come to pass.
For surely your word will give us reason to praise en masse.

Hope changes every trial and tribulation that would drag us down.
For surely you create opportunities to share your thorny crown.

Love changes every withered and parched reed.
For surely fruitfulness comes from your living seed.

Mercy changes every ill-intentioned wrong and failure to act.
For surely the more we are forgiven the stronger our contract.

Grace changes every set of hands that cling to anything, yet nothing. sting/bring/
For surely you portion out your heart, flesh, and every good thing.

Truth changes every dark thought and feeling we harbor in our hearts.
For surely once your light is set in our temples in never ever departs.

Pleasure

Pleasure's trap only the living dead can escape from.
Pleasure's crown only the living sacrifices reject as scum.

Passion swelling while reducing the daily ration.
Appetite enlarging while smothering the oxygen for our light.
Desire growing while strangling the daily prayers sent higher.

The daily scent of our home beyond this life's horizon.
Liberation found in the same box a pilgrim dies in.
The daily glimpse of our eternal image beneath a lifetime of rust.
Identity found in the same breath that outlives our flesh that returns to dust.
The daily melody of our victory crescendo'ing as we near the finish line.
Destiny found in the same unanswered prayer that demanded a sign.
The daily haunting of our divine nature swindled by every shortsighted thought.
Godliness found in the same forbidden fruit that destined humanity to forever rot.

Like a shiver shaking its way down your spine;
Unexpected despite winters chill setting its stage.
Like a sunset stealing your breath with majesty divine;
Unexpected despite dusk's enveloping rampage.
Like a drunken buzz that lifts a heavy heart with wine;
Unexpected despite addiction's tempting cage.

The good in the birds of the sky;
Singing creation's song as they fly.
The good in the beasts of the field;
Filling their native land till Earth be healed.
The good in the plants of the Earth;
Reluctant that men might show their worth.

The good in the starry host spread across the universe;
Testifying to the creator's fingerprint even before the curse.

The good in the water's depths hidden far below;
Man's mysterious backyard reminding them how little they know.
The good in the dirt imbued with God's breath;
God's stewarding idols created to conquer sin and death.

Each invasion of pleasure like a step on heaven's stairway.
Every time we twist nature for our own pleasure like ascending a dune.
Each rising of pleasure's tide like watering hope's seeds hidden away.
Every time we grab hold with both hands like dancing along with folly's tune.
Each current of pleasure fans the flame of desire illuminating heaven's gateway.
Every time we fuel its flame like dousing flesh in gasoline hoping to be immune.

Hinting that satisfaction is just around diligence's corner;
Chasing the shadow of desire toward the substance of hope.

Hinting that fulfillment is just around humility's corner;
Chasing the shadow of pleasure toward the substance of faith.

Hinting that joy is just around ignorance's corner;
Chasing the shadow of happiness toward the substance of love.

Pleasure, the fount of all virtues corrupt and divine.
Intangibly marking heaven and hell's dividing line.
The foundation beneath seasons' perpetual consort.
Pleasantly fluctuating, yet constant enough to comfort.
Hedonism the opposing side to godliness' coin.
Harvesting from the same service one is reluctant to join.
The fount of all virtues divine and corrupt.
Tangibly melding heaven and hell's boundaries abrupt.

Convenient Burden

When home was just around the bend,
And my vagrant life drew near its end.
Homeward the only direction I'd ever had;
Never taking root despite lush soil or comfy pad.

The back road little known and rarely found.
Its entrance in plain sight for those on death's highway bound.
The dirt road home I have coveted for so long.
Death's door just the beginning of another song.

A solitary pilgrim on an endless pilgrimage.
An earthen idol daily losing its maker's image.
Behind the wheel of a large truck;
A seat above others where I was stuck.

The heavy-handed boldness I claimed effective.
The hesitancy that kept grace's hand elusive.
A seat of power filling my tongue with pride and wrath.
A seat of clarity revealing slivers in others along the path.

The rightness that convinced me I needn't budge.
Idleness that let my spirit collect more than a little pudge.
Like a fearless activist stops a tank in its tracks;
Stood two vagabonds with a roadblock of riches at their backs.

A collection diverse enough to offer an apple for every eye.
But just as a bird with a burden could not hope to fly.
A vagabond that pitches his tent in the same place;
With life's subtle breeze cannot hope to keep pace.

Bumper to pedestrian I failed to advance an inch.
My engine revving near their faces yet they didn't flinch.
Complacency an invisible barrier for all who refused to digress.
Vanity Fair firmly established by pilgrims without progress.

Disembarking to cast aside their reason to stay.
To restore a world of black and white by narrowing the gray.

Stopping to clear the pilgrim's path.
For my sake as well as theirs.
Embarking to clean up sin's aftermath.
For even my bleeding heart cares.

How foolish my mind to think I could draw closer to you,
Despite ignoring the towel in your hand.
How foolish my eyes fail to see your kingdom breaking through,
Despite passing by your prodigal strand.
How deceived my heart content to sojourn alone,
Despite countless two-man obstacles.
How deceived my flesh to not notice where you've blown,
Despite my strength bound in shackles.

Surely I was as content to wander on my own,
As they to settle down amidst your path.
Surely many a citizen of Zion overstays in a pit-stop town.
As do those that forget the price of your wrath.

Surely none draw nearer your door whilst ignoring your voice,
Yet every day your door swings wide when you are our choice.

Like the good Samaritan you have always stopped for me.
Like the wicked servant I tend to ignore my brother's plea.
Like the compassionate father your arms are open wide.
Like the elder brother I don't share your heart though I'm at your side.

Between heaven and Earth where I was stuck.
Stuck trying to lift up while being dragged down.
Down to where every destiny has ever changed.
Changed as knees hit Earth and heaven hits home.
Home built in a heart that need never again roam.
Roam restlessly until our burden be exchanged.
Exchanged for the Spirit's fruit and a crown.
Crown You give to those who leave the truck.

Kindred vagrants who downgraded mystery for comfort;
Fellow prodigals who left their inheritance to chase a skirt.
Front line soldiers who had laid down their arms;
Field hands that had abandoned their farms.
Salt that could no longer flavor the world;
Medicine that's taken then quickly hurled.
Lights that could no longer cast darkness aside;
Flames that burned for a night then died.

I knew without their treasures they would continue on their way.
Treasures like shackles and chains bind though little they may weigh.
Just as a little folly is sure to outweigh wisdom,
So hands full of dirt can't lay hold your kingdom.
Just as a little vulnerability negates great strength,
So backsliding can negate advances of any length.

You say to take no extra cloak or purse,
But selfishness clothes me head to toe.
You say to pray for enemies rather than curse,
But turning my cheek leads to another blow.
You say if I look back I'm not worthy to be yours,
But if I look ahead I see an empty cross with my name.
You say we hold the key to heaven's doors,
But I bet it away to break even in life's rigged game.
You say your yolk is easy and your burden is light,
But I collect tools and weapons that I can use to fight.
You say that all who are weary and thirsty should come,
But I scour the earth looking for more because I'm dumb.

Desire, Identity, Destiny, Worship

Desire births Identity for who we were created to be:
Desire begins like a hunger that grumbles after eating your fill,
Desire fulfilled is like the high tide of the sea,
Made perfect when it's the same as His will.

Identity births destiny for what we were created to do,
Identity begins like trying on shoes that could never possibly fit,
Identity fulfilled is like a baby eagle pushed from the nest till away he flew,
Made perfect when our freedom steers the same as the Spirit's bit.

Destiny births worship for what we were created to create,
Destiny begins like a child turning a blizzard into a snowy fort,
Destiny fulfilled is like a Jesus lure with us as the bait,
Made perfect when our every attitude and action begins to exhort.

Desire:
Desire the deepest imprint of our maker that can't be scraped away,
Like a tattoo chosen to wear forever but embedded in a single day,
Desire the 'imago dei' forever setting us apart from all other created beings,
Like a picture of a mountain compared to flying above the Rockies on wings,
Desire the heart's core that precedes the senses,
Refusing to abide within any of life's fences,
Inwardly chosen as much as outwardly bestowed,
Outwardly tested as much as inwardly decoded,
Yet still chosen by a maturing and conscious will,
The restless voice that whispers when the world goes still,
Desire to play the part only you can hope to play,
Desire to say the words only you can say,
The depths of desire taking eternity to search out,
The heart's compass pointing to His intended route,

Identity:

Beginning as the well-made product of a skilled craftsman,

Ensured forever when we cast aside our opinions for our father's grin,

Grafted into the branch of Jesse filled with fruit before we came,

Pruned branches half purged by the winnowing of Jesus' name,

Embraced today but also bestowed before birth,

The price your brother paid determines your worth,

Identity that precedes and transcends actions be they good or ill,

Fighting it is like Sisyphus forever rolling his boulder uphill,

Action rooted in identity like fruit turns to seed, tree, then back to fruit once more,

Embracing it like floating downstream from channel, to river, to vast ocean floor,

An identity not earned nor at stake,

Yet more often than not traded for a fake,

Identity not forced upon us except by being irresistible,

Though easily neglected amidst hoarding all things perishable,

The sinuous deck of cards we're dealt,

Owning faults and strengths always felt,

Bestowed like the design of a snowflake before it falls to the ground,

Like skies that can't be touched even by the highest tree around,

First bestowed to transcend our genes, culture, and race,

Then chosen rooting eternity in our words and deeds of grace,

Chosen like a warrior naturally chooses the blade that best fits his hand,

Becoming an extension of self that puts us on the front of a warring band,

Instilled to transcend fluctuating fancies and covetous dreams,

Embracing it anchors peace though daily corruptive schemes,

The disjointed dots of fate left for us to connect,

Connected by our fumbling toward us made perfect,

By admitting what we are and what we are not,

We find the boundaries of self we have sought,

By denying the endless list of opinions and accusations,
We find the freedom to co-reign with no stipulations,

The sons the sons because the father the father,
The spirit the spirit because the sons in the Son,
The father the father because of the spirit in the sons,

Destiny:
Self-awareness unlocking hands to do what we were made to do,
Releasing us from toiling over work entrusted to others too,
The good deeds planned ahead with our good in mind,
The life-giving process that never turns into a grind,
The role to play that never fits till we take the stage,
Tempting others to leave their self-imprisoned cage,
Like shoes that feel few sizes too large,
Fit better if we haphazardly ahead charge,

Just as a plow is for plowing groves to plant,
So learn from the working and digging ant,
Just as each body part has a role to play,
So learn from others about your unique way,
Surely no hammer was ever made to cut wood,
Yet Jesus abandoned carpentry in his adulthood,
Surely no man was ever made to go with his cultures flow,
Yet Jesus abandoned native lands to help His brothers grow,
Surely no saw was ever made to hammer nails as they stubbornly stood,
Yet Jesus abandoned his right to reign to reveal his father's parenthood,
Surely no woman was ever made to work the soil with a hoe,
Yet Jesus abandoned fertile hearts for kinsmen that sent him below,

The only path never trudged before,
Opened by entering heaven's door,
The only path with no footsteps to follow after,
Opened by the clumsy progress of destiny's drafter,
The only path sure to open our wounds and reveal our scars,
Opened by scattering kingdom seeds instead of personal memoirs,
The only path long enough to walk forever,
Opened by those who fruitless ties can sever,

Worship:
No longer on mountain top nor at temple grand,
But tapping into the ways of our unseen homeland,
No longer with lengthy public prayers and fasting,
But tapping into eternities work forever lasting,
No longer by good intentioned words and deeds,
But tapping into the shepherd's work of plucking at weeds,
No longer pouring out the sacrifice of fools,
But tapping into our creator's invested tools,
A life giving process for us and others,
Love's legacy sustained by its members,
A freedom festering process for us and others,
Love's inheritance freely shared with our brothers,
A confidence building process for us and others,
Love's foundation firm though we blow like feathers,
A heart expanding process for us and for others,
Love's appreciation for fleeting fleshly flowers,

Impossible to pour out as much as pours in,
Inevitable that it overrides our nature of sin,
Impossible to never set foot on its untrodden path,
Inevitable that it daily immerse in the Spirits bath,

Impossible to worship without being fruitful,
Inevitable that it meet your father's approval,
Created naively amidst pleasure then maintained amidst fruitless leisure,
Born bloody amidst spiritual wars then laid to rest as the defeated lion roars,
Discovered unexpectedly amidst a minefield then infecting every day we yield,
Walked out stubbornly amidst an enticing crowd
suggesting you relax in darkness' shroud,

Each soul's unique entrance to his throne,
Another cast aside rock becoming a living stone,
Each soul's unique entrance into his pastures green,
Another cast aside portrait needing to be seen,
Each soul's unique entrance for the sap from the Elder vine,
Another cast aside crumb left that the humble might dine,
Each soul's unique entrance to glories leaving a groove for others to follow after,
Another cast aside detour sure to produce the most precious thing, God's laughter,

Our will's entrance to his ways;
Enjoying how the Spirit clears our haze.
Our mind's entrance to His thoughts;
Enjoying the Spirit's buzz like heavenly shots.
Our heart's entrance to His feelings;
Enjoying the Spirit's overflow causing healings.
Our sense's entrance to taste of him;
Enjoying how the Spirit fills us to the brim.
Our nature's entrance made new by homeward ruts;
Enjoying how the Spirit prunes destiny with heart cuts.

Unknowable Friends

Disbelieve demons and they are sure to stab you in the back.
Give attention to demons and you'll find power they never lack.
Disbelieve angels and they may stand against you but always with the Lord.
Give attention to angels and you may miss out on the good they hoard.

"You are in error because you do not know the scriptures."
The son of man destined to act through the ages leaving fleshly pictures.
"You are in error because you do not know the power of God."
The son man destined to see shortcomings underfoot thoroughly trod.
"At the resurrection people with neither marry nor be given in marriage."
The son of man's desire destined to outlast any matrimonial bondage.
"But when the dead rise they shall be like the angels in heaven."
The son of man destined to rise (though creation bake) like bread with leaven.

The diligent helpers of man whose service often goes unappreciated.
Representing a reign as passive as active but with victory already fated.
The messengers bringing plague or revelation remain untamed.
Representing division among even their own with prides maimed.
The stainless gears that turn with God's every advance.
Representing an invasion postponed to give mercy a chance.
The transient thrill-seekers catching us up in adventures yet to unfold.
Representing destinies already formed in eternity's future as if of old.
The frolicking sprites singing joyful songs that to earthly ears remain unheard.
Representing heaven's greatest scandal whose ripples still seem absurd.
The empathetic brothers steeling into my solitary room of sorrows unseen.
Representing a father's graceful arms, sure to outlast discipline for his teen.
The majestic beauties regularly taking pity on our needs unmet.
Representing communication's climax that alone you'll never get.

The fearless comrades shielding lives yet remaining unknown.
Representing his kingdom's training wheels that are out on loan.

How much of our fruitfulness comes from their labor?
While amongst ourselves trivialities we belabor.
How much of our peace comes from their diligence?
While amongst ourselves we spread fires of ambivalence.
How much of our pleasure comes from their humble service?
While amongst ourselves our petty agendas grow rampant with malice.
How much of our success comes from their warring for our hearts?
While amongst ourselves we compare to have better looks or smarts.
How much of our health comes from them tending to our frail flesh?
While amongst ourselves we hope to grind others under us like a thresh.
How much of our inspiration comes from their hinting whispers?
While amongst ourselves our subtle grace resembles crashing bumpers.
How much of our uprightness comes from their supporting our swaying branches?
While amongst ourselves the taller one grows the more savage its peers' scratches.

No memory could hold onto their every intercession;
Intercession soon forgotten no matter how divine the session.
No mortal frame could withstand the strain of their daily duty;
Duty soon revealing frail fleshly hearts that often covet their beauty.
No lowly service could come close to their pure-hearted aid;
Aid soon elevating humble men to dangerously high seats that fade.
No human heart could endure the times their hands are tied;
Tied as soon as fallen man entertain that God withholds or has lied.

The angelic hunger to taste of a hardship tempered holy heart.
Meeting the human desire for our best to be known from the start.
The angelic ministry to those in a desolate land.
Meeting the spirit's children when they can hardly stand.

The angelic glory considered rubbish yet enthralled by his imprinted image.
Meeting hapless souls that are an accident away from death's carnage.
The angelic strength that has never known weakness or fear.
Meeting sickly and fearful vessels daring to hope as his words they hear.
The angelic battle-hardened vanguards loyal to only one son of man.
Meeting at best prideful children seeking glory along their shortsighted plan.
The angelic armies that care not if our allegiance remains undecided.
Meeting superstitious idolaters performing as if with devotion undivided.
The angelic creations of light that are eternally self-sufficient.
Meeting the ceaselessly deficient shells that house the omniscient.
The angelic witnesses that can recall his reign prior to the divine scandal.
Meeting the adopted children reared as brothers though unworthy to untie his sandal.

Perhaps they were made as much for us as for him.
Their care for your needs is never compulsory.
Our ignorance propagates the self-sabotaging story.
Their care for your needs is always optional.
Our ignorance would equate their service as conjugal.
Perhaps we were made as much for them as for him.

Apathy and Amnesia

Apathy like a serpent's neurotoxin;
Numbing you just long enough to devour you whole.
Amnesia like a tattoo needle sinking deep into the skin;
Numbing your destiny without even touching your soul.

Every lifeless idol spreads their poison.
Every second glance or lasting gaze our sin.
Your greatest obstacle in this life is within.
Your greatest triumph in this life found without.
Daily repentance the only entrance to freedom's route.
Every living thing drinking from the same living fount.

No army can rival the threat they pose;
Bringing nations low daily without breaking a sweat.
No disaster can compare to their casualties and fatal blows;
Torturing every generation skilled at spreading crippling throes.
No friendship can endure their pressure like an unpaid debt;
Tearing strong homes apart as fast as tornadoes.

Till the sun's light no longer reaches your eyes.
Till the son's voice be just another echo pestering like flies.
Till the sun's warmth no longer reaches your flesh.
Till the son's spirit with yours can no longer mesh.

Adjusted to darkness your eyes won't bear the light of life.
Adjusted to cold your skin cringes at warmth as from a scalding knife.
Then darkness without will open your heart to sin,
And the void of eternity match the cavity within.

Apathy like a cozy roadside coffin along a restless journey
Will bury you alive before you wake from your reprieve.
Apathy like a mortician dressed as an EMT wheeling your gurney.
Only the blind and the living dead will they deceive.

Apathy like a blind man behind the wheel.
Like leprous skin, even death's touch it cannot feel.
Men lacking the sense that distinguishes them from beast.
Like charity replaced by exploitation from a corrupt priest.

Apathy like a sheltering cave whose mouth collapses overnight;
Sure to hide you from even the brightest dawn's light.

Amnesia will daily drag you down;
Under an ocean of troubles.
Like trying to swim in a baggy gown;
Your existence amounting to a few lonely bubbles.

Amnesia like slipping from slumber into a coma.
A coma that robs you of your future along with your past trauma.
Like a harmless slip that sends you over a perilous ledge.
A ledge along a bottomless pit no one will dare attempt to dredge.
Like a doctor's promise of health to a patient on death's door.
A one-way door sending you to settle judgment's score.
Like a negligent anesthesiologist letting your heartbeat fade along with your pain.
A fading pain whose sensation you will mourn while apathy's comfort you gain.

Amnesia like thick coastal fog blanketing a sleeping world in gray.
Fuddling your mind from the scars and lessons of yesterday.
Hiding the snares and thorns littering every winding path.
Hiding the truth that your path leads to certain wrath.

Fuddling your mind with anxiety no matter where your head may lay.
Amnesia obscuring frequent exits along death's highway.

Apathy a convincing coach offering retirement prior to your prime.
Amnesia a thief stealing forgotten treasures one at a time.
Apathy like being cursed with a foreign tongue.
Amnesia like being sent to a foreign land when young.
Apathy like being stuck in your own dream with no control.
Amnesia like daily waking from a blacked-out night will waste away your soul.

Apathy like an unopened bottle of pills promises your sorrow to drown.
Amnesia like an upturned liquor bottle in your mouth while you lie down.
Apathy like hidden poison in a pet's feeding trough.
Amnesia like a nightcap that never comes off.

Greater the threats that reside within the fence.
Your heart's fence locking your foe in and your friends out.
Trivial the quakes and wars that forever rage about.
Perilous apathy's embrace and amnesia's ceaseless incense.

They have taken more captives than any war or plague.
Never releasing prisoners no matter how loud you beg.
Violated more innocents than any slave trade.
No agency can halt their spreading corruption with a raid.

They have created more fools than any addiction.
Lured more to death's highway than any bestselling fiction.
Snuffed more flickering flames then a winter storm that douses a campfire.
Severed more bent reeds than all mankind's advances destined to backfire.

To Die Or Not To Die, That's The Question

To die or not to die,
To die to yourself you must be ready to live for others,
But you'll never be ready till you try,
Guarding your life turns many demons into lovers.

To live or not to live,
Seeking eternal life will lead you to the grave,
To live from Heaven's shores, you must be a native,
Abandon the life you know to find the life you crave.

Sin

Sin, the itch that lives in the skin;
Our enemy that lives under the same roof.
Sin, the duplicity squatting within;
Our enemy's rotten fruit the visible proof.

Sin lurks at our doorstep waiting to master the unaware;
To hijack our temple and turn it into a condemned lair.
An open heart is a one-way entrance for him.
There's no getting him to leave till you turn grim.

Sin's irritable itch proportional to our idleness.
Peace-less busyness and peace-less stillness.
The spinning wheel behind this world's grand rat race;
Preoccupying some and grinding others leaving no trace.

A two-faced coin you flip to escape blame;
Sending you farther from truth's doorway.
A little rule bending to win a single game;
Sending you along death's broad highway.
A pet lizard that turns into a man-eating dragon;
Sending you into its jowls with your tail a wag'in.

The plank protruding from your own eye,
That focuses on your brother's speck.
Others' shortcomings always easy to spy.
Our own filth rotting just beneath the deck.

The burden that hinders our helping hand,
Because we've torn away from the spirit's strand.
The thorny snares about your feet you think to be roots,
Because you admired those with fruitful earthen shoots.

Controlling your world by manning hell's flood gates;
Daily damming your heart's waters with rocks and weights.
Controlling heartache's out-pour by stopping the source;
Daily forsaking your destiny by choosing today's course.
Twisting the greater by controlling the lesser;
Daily grappling with fate like a wounded wrestler.
Appeasing the devil by displeasing the lord;
Daily cowering before a shadow that roared.

Sin, entering through one man's naivety.
Atoned for by one man's sacrificial piety.

Sin, gripping our lives while in the womb we're curled.
The age-old arms welcoming us into this world.

Sin, your irresistible habit used to manage anxiety.
Addiction replacing addiction never tasting sobriety.

Sin, as resilient as roaches infesting your septic.
Merely surviving will turn you into a skeptic.

Sin, missing the mark with word and deed.
Taking after our father Adam's fallen seed.

Sin, the apple in Eve's eye.
Distorted by a serpent's lie.

Sin, the snake's venom spreading within.
The one thing that makes Satan grin.

Sin, the unknown we traded Earth's reign for;
Forfeiting also our right to enter heaven's door.

Sin, not doing the good you ought to do;
Looking on as dark times festered and grew.

Sin, the life insurance that provides a coffin;
Relinquishing your first fruits to pay for often.

Sin, like desert weeds that thrive in any soil;
The yeast that makes your daily bread spoil.

Sin, the age-old enslaver of men;
Swindling nine out of every ten.

Sin, sure to leave you missing destiny's mark;
Your trajectory obscured by eternities dark.

The insatiable pit of desire in your gut;
Daily diverting your destiny into a rut.

The unquenchable fire in your lap;
Daily smudging heaven's road map.

The bittersweet fruit that leaves you craving more;
Daily supplanting pleasure with an all too familiar bore.

The twisting of creation for our own pleasure or use;
Daily torn from the living vine as a fruitless spruce.

Mourning to Joy

In the delivery room we gathered to mourn.
Mourn my bride's loss of self as our child was born.
Born as the father of all fathers turned our mourning into joy.
Joy as my beloved's lost identity came back for us to enjoy.

As a dream comes with many cares;
So heaven reveals its intended pairs.
As a heavy heart comes from hoping too long;
So I stretch & fray the longer things go wrong.
As peace comes after paying the price of war;
So my heart could only trust after in half it tore.
As your word comes true despite our old age;
So hope stalls as you set redemption's stage.

After years searching for the girl of my dreams;
Elusive joy that appeared to join in heaven's schemes.
After years trying to make whimsical flings last;
Heat-less coals whose flames belong in the past.
After years making peace with my deficiencies;
Buying into your vision by abandoning contingencies.
After years carving out my destiny alone;
I see beauty shares my hidden fate and bone.

The heart of my heart saved via childbirth;
Only after my hopes lay to rest in dearth.
The hope of my hope found after being lost;
Only after mourning turned to joy at no cost.
The fear of my fear sprawled out for me to bear;
Only after I fall under the load do I value your care.

Though I tried, I could find no fault in her beauty;
Loving her as I've been loved an effortless duty.
Though I cried, I could find no comfort in her loss;
Watching my partner overcome by amnesia's dross.
Though I lied, I could not find the heart to raise our child on my own;
Embracing a heartless fate with all my heart as a father bitterly grown.

My hardened eyes couldn't help but soften before her smile;
As her memory momentarily returned after a long while.
My calloused heart couldn't help but soften before her gaze;
Though her light would soon fade within forgetfulness' maze.
My sharpened tongue couldn't help but soften before her kiss;
Sharing her best with me to the very end that I might taste bliss.
My stable mind couldn't help but quake before her loss of self;
A trophy wife torn away to be a hollow image setting on the shelf.

When it was too late you turned our mourning into joy,
And my faith was born newer than our infant boy.
When it was too late to stop tragedy from eclipsing our son's birth,
And my gift of new life was neither wife nor child but of inner worth.
When it was too late you returned my lost heart,
And my delight in you grew deeper than at the start.
When it was too late to stop the flow of sorrowful tears,
And my newfound joy kept the flow as you dispelled my fears.

Happiness

Happiness was yours like a virgin bride;
Till your eyes saw fruit you hadn't tried;
Till your heart and will left reason behind.
Her departure leaving you emotionally blind.

The tighter your grip the sooner through your hands she'll slip.
The longer for her you seek the farther away she will sneak.
The more often you see her face the fewer tracks she'll leave to trace.
The more traps you lay for her the more frequent her retreats will occur.
The greater the longing for her touch the more severe
you'll limp from crutch to crutch.

She's chased from shore to shore more often than any skirt;
Forever elusive despite countless days on this world of dirt.
She's chased longer than the most ambitious dream;
Forever coveted though her favor will never redeem.

Seasoned hunters abandon native lands hoping to pin her down;
While destitute revelers turn from her and face the thorny crown.
She has shown herself in the most obvious of places;
In countless children's naive laughs and soft faces.

Like a good friend that is carried far away by life;
Like youth's crush that never intended to be a wife.
I let her carry out her business that took her far away;
Knowing wisdom could not come if she were to stay.

Each of wisdom's lessons will loosen her hold on your heart;
Just as oil is destined to rise above water and remain apart.

Each of life's lessons will extract from happiness' traces left behind;
Just as termites eat away at roots till only a cavity you will find.

She departs in the night like a jaded lover;
Leaving no clue or trail for you to uncover.
Then the game master realizes he's just another pawn;
Leaving you to wake without her warmth at the crack of dawn.

When she has gone you will feel a different man;
Like the aftermath of a dying idol for a devoted fan.
You'll wake from bliss' drunken stupor lost and alone;
At the best you will find a substitute to call bone of your bone.

At worst your capstone-less home will become condemned in time;
You'll slumber as your rafters sag to drown in visions of your prime.
You will be deceived to think yourself less than before;
Like a mourning parent that outlives the child they adore.

Forever hidden right under your self-centered nose;
As untraceable as the eastern wind that blows.
Like an irreplaceable friend visiting from afar;
Bittersweet the reunion prior to even seeing their car.

Her unexpected departure will leave you dead in your tracks;
Like a pauper at his wedding feast not knowing what he lacks.
Like waking from a drunken stupor lost and alone;
A fleshly heart fated to become harder than stone.

Like training wheels teach the fearful to ride;
So she comes from above in love's ways for us to guide.
Like a climber's rope whose presence sustains a weary hope;
Keeping courage burning long enough to ascend sorrow's slope.

Surely there's more happiness in a child's shallow smile;
Than a grinning CEO sitting smugly atop the world.
Surely more of her among those who walk the extra mile;
Than a well fed snake upon itself forever curled.

Surely she leaves behind the pearls we toss to swine;
As we seek her in a deep bottle or a well-aged wine.
Surely more of her likeness in a newborn's puffy face;
As we set the stage for them to enter the same rigged race.

As for me I sought her not;
Tempted rather by her elder sister.
Thus I avoided being caught;
Following the footsteps of many a minister.

When she is gone you will feel a different creature;
Like a student left to his own devices by his teacher.
As much as a caterpillar wakes from its cocoon changed;
A glimpse of bliss vanishes lest you walk as one deranged.

You will be convinced to think yourself less than before;
Like confident souls are ravaged by the cruelty of war.
Deceived to believe your life has become a trivial mess;
Resignation foretells your checkmate in life's game of chess.

She is like a friend visiting from afar;
You can only delay her departure.
For no man is born under her star;
But every soul scared by her torture.

Her coming and going as natural as the ocean's tides;
Even among her King's offspring she flees and hides.
Both her coming and going serve his purpose;
In the end both joy and sorrow work for us.

Her presence like a feast meant to lighten hearts and strengthen hands;
Her absence tipping the scales for pilgrims in favor of unknown lands.
She'll enter your heart's door like love's twin,
And walk out before her favor you can win.

Soon his world opens as we learn to walk on our own;
Letting go his helping hand to steward all he has grown.

Single

When the sun rises, a lonely tree is never in the dark.
Every day it offers its shade to every sojourning lark.
When the sun sets, a lonely owl has its pick of prey.
Every day it hoots a pleasant song till the first light of day.
When the storm passes, a lonely house stands undamaged.
Every day it turns strangers into a family if properly managed.
When trouble comes, a lonely heart braces itself and plunges on.
Every day it shares its unreserved warmth until it is all gone.

Even a lonely dog is better off than a king with harem in tow,
because there is nothing hindering the spirit's flow.
Even a lonely lily is better off than a dozen roses,
because it won't wither far from the sun in vases.
Even a lonely boy is better off than married man,
because he wakes every day available to God's plan.

A single-minded man is like a bulldozer plowing adversity.
A single vision among family or community sustains unity.
A single affirmation can heal years of neglect or abuse.
A single change of heart can halt a long war with a truce.
A single revelation can bring a lifetime of clarity and vision.
A single desire, to be with the one who died and has risen.

Death Indiscriminate

Death Indiscriminate...
No longer working at the base of a vast burning pit,
But bins upon bins filled by as many thralls as could fit.
Forever fulfilling his task from the preeminent.

Death, he was neither good nor bad.
But gloated over every corpse to add.
But to those raised his delight seems oddly sad,
For death never worked alongside redemption's dad.

Not fair to call his murderous intent demonic;
Not fitting to call his godly commission angelic.

Who am I that I should rise from among the slain?
Who am I to walk away as your heart beats in my chest?
Only after there is no blood left to fill a single vein.
Only after tasting the bitter fate of all that fail life's test.

Relieved death took no notice of my escape I trudged on;
Till death's cat sentry sunk its claws deep in my leg.
Singing pain clawed up skin leaving my senselessness gone.
Feline eyes wide as I defied my deserved fate; not having to beg.

The father having bequeathed his son to death's merciless clutch;
Likewise, did not spare me from death's brutal touch.
Like a child before a sadistic doctor with massive needle in hand;
Death's weapon cleaved every visitor imprinting his justice brand.

Sorting the dead from the living with death;
Glad to take center stage in the harvest of souls.

Sorting the life of his kids by taking their breadth;
Glad to administer sin's toll and sever the fate it controls.

Silence there was a haunting echo of tragedy never laid to rest;
Despair a piercing noise smothering both mind and heart.
Like a gag stuffed so far down breath ceases in your chest;
Rotten fruit made ripe as destined from the very start.

Death was still rejoicing in my slaughter at his hands;
As I took one last look behind, then ventured to parts unknown.
Forever free from his clutch as well as torment's brands;
Distance from death growing with each heavenly breeze blown.

Thousands had fallen as he slew his way to me and now his joy made him drunk;
Like a woodsman clearing weeds and thorns to get to his prized hardwood trunk.
A thousand generations more feared the fate he had in store,
And ironically sinned their way closer to his door.

My life the prize he coveted most;
Like a taster samples his way through the bland to savor the exquisite.
Stumbling over countless cold and shifting limbs that hoped for a new host;
Shifting like a tick sensing life but painful to the touch like a zit.

Not knowing where I was headed,
But certain death was behind for good.
Leaving behind many things I had long dreaded;
Even a cross with my name etched in the wood.

Divine Assembly Defense

A great hall packed with angels and siblings of great renown;
Not an obscure member gathered from among and beyond Zion town.
A question was raised from embittered lungs;
Doubts and accusations rose from governing tongues.
The ruling heir letting their fires grow by being absent;
About his father's business, but not needing to be sent.
To question his goodness is to fuel all kinds of doubt.
Forsaking the sustainer of hope; many fountains ran out.

One by one groups of critiques vanished;
Zion's ruling council taken and perhaps banished.
One by one groups' slander turned into carnal fear;
Zion's ruling council not speaking well of their savior dear.

Questioning his goodness in slew of scandalous reports,
Yet he did not appear to dispel their doubtful retorts.
Questioning his scandalous grace yet again,
Yet he had graciously put into their hands Zion's reign.
Questioning his preferred method of leadership,
Yet he did not clear out this temple with a whip.
Questioning his fearsome discipline that seemed to be overkill,
Yet he only spirited away those who spurned his father's will.
Questioning his instigation of our peace as well as unease,
Yet he can't sit idly by when his father's work undone he sees.
Questioning his character as if he were not his father's son,
Yet he let me speak on his behalf as if his defense was done.
Questioning his frivolous roaming to and fro,
Yet he still follows wherever the spirit may blow.

Questioning his tendency to make obscure hearts a priority,
Yet he was the one that pulled us from sin's curse and obscurity.

Surely he is not that kind of man;
To get even at those unworthy of his lands.

Surely he is not that kind of man;
To destroy the work of his own hands.

Surely he is not that kind of man;
To forget his mercy toward illegitimate strands.

Surely he is not that kind of man;
To be haphazard with a house of cards that on his rock stands.

Only by the trail of impossibilities that flowed from his wake
Could you guess where he had appeared for his father's sake.

Just as the ripples follow after a rock that splashes into calm water;
So could you tell his intervention by hearts escaping sin's slaughter.

By my last word only a tenth of the assembly remained;
Each with clothes and hearts by wearisome tears stained.

Surely there was no bias in his mercy nor his wrath;
His blood enables and hinders our receiving all he hath.

Thousands of earnest lips speak of the absence of tears above our skies,
But all eternity could not halt the flow of fluid sorrow from my eyes.

Thousands of good intentions claim the creator's heart will be known,
But even in God's heavenly home, kingdom seeds have not fully grown.

Questions

Question the world and you will find God.
Question God and you will find yourself.
Question yourself and you will find brokenness.

Question the world and you will find God.
Answering the world like falling into traps hidden by earthen sod.
Avoid worldly traps by bearing blows from his staff and rod.

Question God and you will find yourself.
Answering God like perusing wisdom's bookshelf.
Avoid God and man becomes just another beast himself.

Question yourself and you will find brokenness.
Answering yourself ensures a snake's echo will hiss.
Avoid yourself and healing's whisper you will miss.

Every question a key designed to open a door;
With hidden glories and trials in store.
Those who ask more questions will walk through more doors;
And walk the divide of heaven's shores.
Failing to ask questions puts the key in another's hands,
And locks you away in eternity's scorching grandstands.
Every wise question like a child's innocence that prevails any debate;
Every foolish question like a restless hunter that can't bear to wait.
Just as unanswerable questions teach more than any lecture;
So unhealed wounds stretch skin until scars change their texture.
Just as unresolved sorrow achieves more peace than any war;
So unfulfilled hope offers to leave the heart bigger than before.

Though there are road maps to guide your course through life,
Only questions can help you navigate through sorrow and strife.

Though history reveals wisdom's course new and old,
Only questions can lead to truth's treasures untold.

Only humans have an endless list of why's;
Look to the sparrow or ant to learn lessons lost.
Only humans dare to critique the world with their cries;
Even our ability to be dissatisfied came at a great cost.

Questions always begin with fallen reality;
They grow with unsatisfied desire.
Questions only end when his face we see;
They shrink as we ascend higher.

Questions are like wind to the sails of a boat;
Foretelling either pleasant skies or raging storm.
Questions are like a vest that keeps you afloat;
Foretelling attempts to make your heart conform.

It may be the pumping of blood that runs your body,
But it's questions that keep your spirit's pump beating.
Without them your travels are sure to be short or shoddy;
Perplexing and cruel will be your creator's final meeting.

But don't think your crashing world warrants his response;
His silence is more significant than man's renaissance.
There is only one response to your question of why;
For you to know his grieved heart as a son, not a spy.

Every question like directions for a wayward traveler;
Leading the inquiring heart to sojourn many a hidden paradise.
Seclusion teaching you that death is the universal leveler;
To him and his kin questions are like a pleasing aroma of burned spice.

Do Not Arouse Love

Do not arouse or awaken love until it so desires;
Like all good things she comes and goes as she sees fit.
Like all good things she comes and goes for saints and liars;
Do not arouse or expect her warmth till her candle is lit.

Like any fleeting breeze she passes through independent of your qualms;
Certain to cause the highs and lows David spoke of in his psalms.
Like any fluid she passes through your whitened knuckles;
Certain to undermine your senses like ripened honeysuckles.
Like any caring friend she's willing to come by daily;
Certain to linger among those who welcome her lazily.
Like any stranger she never was and never will be yours;
Certain to stay clear of hearts that are like revolving doors.
Like any invested coach she'll meet you bruised in your corner;
Certain to part with your towel even should you turn family to mourner.
Like any overlooked friend she'll sneak out on momentous days;
Certain to leave behind hollowed vessels covered in earthen glaze.
Like any lost love she departs before you could ever think her a bother;
Certain to steer you away from her and toward your heavenly father.

Romance is at her best when free of chains and obligations;
Love's touch the only hope to change hearts across the nations.
Romance is at her place like the sun even on stormy days;
Love's warmth comes to those who press through life's maze.
Romance is the depth beneath the foam we prize;
Love's shadow-hand remains elusive despite our cries.

Oh passionate one, when will your hate of injustice rival your swooning passion?
With a cause contagious as a flu; what happened to
being content with your daily ration?

Oh stubborn one, when will your perspective be bigger than your stubbornness?
With a heart as hard as stone; what happened to the seed sown despite your dryness?
Oh committed one, when will you value the course as much as your commitment?
With a goal lofty and noble; what happened to being guided by the spirit's every hint?
Oh halfhearted one, when will you conform to Jesus rather than being lukewarm?
With a hat for each season; what happened to your uniqueness that spites the norm?
Oh lazy one, when will the sight of the storm quicken your heavy hand?
With a barn filled to the brim; what happened when death came before you planned?

Do not set out for romance's peak without guidance;
Lest you return empty handed in disappointed silence.
Do not wake desire's dragon from its slumber;
Lest you be lit up like a meaty piece of lumber.
Do not cast your heart away on her endless seas;
Lest you forsake her watering of your fruitless trees.
Do not expect love's throes when you set her stage;
Lest you entrap yourself in a delusional cage.
Do not wait by the door or phone till she falls in your lap;
Lest you overlook friends that will help you close the gap.
Do not follow a beautiful stranger's claim of her touch;
Lest your heart become a platter for vultures and such.
Do not think to place her on display on a shelf or in a vase;
Lest you hasten her withering by removing her from her place.
Do not take her favor for granted by taking her object for yourself;
Lest your exploits amount to selfishness' trophies on a shelf.
Do not think to coax or sway her coming and going;
Lest your schemes clog up her waters from flowing.

His selfless love your only chance to have a change of heart;
His unconditional love your only choice if you value your heart.

Yahweh Our Love

Though Yahweh our love,
You expose our deepest self to all heaven above.
Though Yahweh our life,
You let the world have its way with your wife.
Though Yahweh our one and only,
You watch as our sins die slowly.

Making wisdom my one wish;
You make sorrow my dish.
Making love my heart's desire;
You make me cast my lovers on the pyre.
Making your body the apple of my eye;
You make its fruit fall, rot, and die.

Enticing me with unconditional love;
Then delivering me with your law.
Enticing me with a clean slate;
Then delivering me from forgetfulness.
Enticing me with your promised land;
Then delivering me with an endless pilgrimage.
Enticing me with your peace and rest;
Then delivering me from my slumber.
Enticing me with the fruit of your spirit;
Then delivering me from missing the giver.
Enticing me with your glorious day;
Then delivering me from living for tomorrow.
Enticing me with freedom that moves as the wind;
Then delivering me by sinking my roots deep.

Surely Yahweh our love;
The comforter wrapped around us like a glove.
Surely Yahweh our life;
Pruning me with a double-edged knife.
Surely Yahweh our one and only;
Never again to be lost or lonely.

Prodigal, Elder, Compassionate Father

Prodigals' paths follow every whim of heart;
Spurning wisdom's call from the very start.

Elder brothers' paths follow the status quo;
Taking for granted their father's gracious outflow.

Compassionate fathers' paths follow after the lord;
Having inherited the heart of the maker they adored.

God says he loves us and does so forever.
We claim our love could last a thousand years,
Then tear down love's object to follow after our peers.
God's cords of love; no power of heaven or hell can sever.

When I am the prodigal you send the bill that leaves me destitute;
Destitute as a foreigner surrounded by natives of folly's root.

When I am the elder brother your compassion proves me stingy;
Stingy as an heir whose position and role remains fringy.

When I am the compassionate father you seat me at your table;
Table to dine of and reign in your kingdom that's better than any fable.

Ticks on my Heart 🌿

Days go by;
My body and mind grow tired.
My greatest desire is to die.
Days hold nothing but attacks on how I'm wired.
I live to love, yet never will I love to live.
I give pieces of myself away;
A friend I can't even see is my only motive.
A servant like me; I look for every day.
I am told my face should shine,
And my words bring life to those among the dead.
I should rejoice; instead I constantly whine,
And I only have peace when on my bed.
I am worn out by my many prayers; Surely you are weary of my nagging voice.
Surely you will continue to ignore my many tears.
I am not willing to argue; in the end I have no choice.

To steal, kill, and destroy 🌿

The accuser comes to steal, kill, and destroy;
To steal the seeds of truth scattered about your path;
To kill hope in its infancy by any means or ploy;
To destroy every blooming shoot or taint fruit for wrath.

The son of man comes to seal, kill, and destroy;
To steal the shame that repels you from your fellow man;
To kill the sin lurking behind your fleshly human decoy;
To destroy death so the son of man might embody God's plan.

The Storyteller

If there was ever an answer to the whys of the world;
Surely it is found in the story of heaven's rebellion unfurled.
If there is ever to be repentance in the heart of an adult;
Surely it is found in the story of Adam and Eve's insult.
If there will ever be an end to man's fruitless labor and toil;
Surely it is found in the story of Jesus, for sin's curse he did foil.
If there is ever to be comfort for the lonely and lost;
Surely it is found in Joseph's story if we but count the cost.
If there will ever be insight that extends beyond science's reach;
Surely it is found in the story of an unseen kingdom's breach.
If there is ever to be acceptance of our weaknesses and difficulties;
Surely it can be found in David's story of obedience despite hostilities.

Few are foolish enough to deny that the world is fueled by stories.
Stories that let us escape, then face reality; hopeful of new glories.
Few are wise enough to admit that there must also be a storyteller.
Storyteller whose script began in a garden and began anew in death's cellar.
Few are content enough to avoid trying to write their own script.
Script dictated by a covetous heart; sure to descend toward death's crypt.
Few are ignorant enough to not wander beyond their pasture fence.
Fence dividing Heaven from Earth by traversing every heart; buoyant or dense.
Few are perceptive enough to realize Plato's cave only ever offers artificial light.
Light casting our shade on the wall; that we might
forever shadowbox for divine right.

If your children needed a dreadful foe to value your house, what might you do?
Would you let a snake sneak into your garden, if its intent you fully knew?
If your lover got lost en route to you every time, how might you reunite?

Would you send your servants to show the way if
she always retreated from their sight?
If you took on the same flesh as the people you set apart, could you be their guide?
Would you bear with the whitewashed tombs and dens
of robbers that were to be your bride?
If your bride followed after every suitor that came
by, how might you rekindle her love?
Would you seek the harlot out and redeem her, hoping
she learn to live as pure as a dove?
If the daughter of your youth was taken to a foreign land, would you dare invade?
Would you risk the glory of your house on one son's obedience; his own life to trade?

The more simple the truth, the more all-encompassing it can be.
Surely the alpha and omega loves a good story just as much as we.
The more convoluted our attempts to make sense of things, the greater our naiveté.
Surely the story of every son of man began and ended on resurrection Sunday.

If we are made in God's image, then surely he shares our love for stories.
Yet just like an RPG, no one who enjoys playing can bear to simply observe them.
If we are made of God's lineage, then surely our
stories extend to heavenly territories.
Yet just like a tall tale, no one expected the creator to take center stage in Bethlehem.

Though there is no remembrance of men of old,
Every man of worth leaves a tale that future generations will be told.
Though history has always been written by the victors,
Every man of worth handles with care, the hope of the survivors.
Though there is nothing genuinely new under the sun,
Every man of worth finds a way to be creative and have fun.
Though there is less truth in a legend the longer it endures,
Every man of worth leaves the world changed as he matures.

Though nothing can be added to or taken away from creation,
Every man of worth finds a way to rise above his given station.

To the grand historian, every instructive parable is non-fiction.
To the author and sustainer of faith, every broken heart is his jurisdiction.
To the tolerator of original sin, every birth embodies redemption of man's treason.
To the inventor of union, every budding romance blooms and withers in season.
To the record keeper and judge, man's achievements and faults are trite.
To the king of scandals, even adopted bastards qualify for divine right.

Even the trials of a good story seem preferable to our boring reality.
Even the persecution of a revolutionary seems better than our obscurity.
Even the shattered hope of a visionary seems more admirable than our defeatism.
Even the fanciful notions of a romantic seem grand compared to our realism.
Even the sorrow of the shunned inspires compassion of they turn to suicide.
Even the fear of a coward seems acceptable if he survives to turn the tide.

Cleaved

When death cleaves your soul from flesh what of you will remain?
We call 'real' our self that will be tossed out like a garment with a stain.

When life cleaves your new nature from sinful nature, how much of you endures?
We call 'fate' our unrefined will that has caused each one of our fruitless detours.

When eternity cleaves your stewardship from fantasies, how much do you have left?
We call 'destiny' our entrusted talents that reveal
(without grace) we are forever bereft.

He calls reliable and true all that passes through death unscathed.
He calls us to remain holy and distinct though the world be depraved.

Look at your body, how much control do you have of your own health?
Designed to be part of a larger body sharing of each member's wealth.

Inspect the hairs on your head, can you turn a single gray?
Designed to change color or fall out as a warning we decay.

Monitor your thoughts, how often are they steered as you see fit?
Designed to reveal all that incubates the heart of each hypocrite.

Look at your life, how many circumstances bend to your will?
Designed to put you on your knees after exhausting all your skill.

Lift your gaze to the horizon, how can you halt or hasten the sun's rising?
Designed to share its light with the good and wicked while daily galvanizing.

Marinotha

Every great son and daughter of the lord was sure;
Sure the day of his return would soon bring the cure.
Cure death, disease, and darkness till all creation be pure.
Every lowly son and daughter thought their time was vast;
Vast enough to accommodate their fancies of reliving the past.
Past dead and gone, yet tainting their days to the very last.
Every great son and daughter knew they must finish their work;
Work during the day before the sun sets abruptly with irk.
Irk unless we finish illuminating and shaming the powers that lurk.
Every lowly son and daughter thought their work was for pay;
Pay that entitled them to hoard and spend on their frivolous play.
Play out self-gratification's course rather than repent and pray.

Soon the mourning bell will toll for thee.
As the setting sun is the most glorious;
Soon the sun will set before thee.
As the prodigal returns home victorious;
Soon the rifles will shout for thee.
As the fair weathered friends gather once more;
Soon the veiled faces mark tale's end for thee.
As the regret and joy stream down the faces we adore;
Soon the treasured man cave will lay absent of thee;
As the flesh covered work you ignored moves on.
Soon the hoarded treasures be distributed for thee;
As the crowd at your back pushes as death calls anon.

If you don't finish your work today, it'll be left to forever decay.
Left as all your hopes return with you to this world's clay.
If you don't press your luck to carve out a destiny as his, it'll set as is.

Set as unfinished sculpture; forever revealing your score on life's quiz.
If you don't see it coming, you'll think I'm simply bluffing.
Think your world secure though the lord be scuffing.
If you don't take heed, you'll never shake free of your naive greed.
Shake loose your settling for less though toward new glories he will lead.
If you don't brace yourself as a man, you'll blow farther from his glorious plan.
Blow on the whims and waves of the times every day of your short lifespan.

My neighbor finished his long-desired workshop then a month later passed;
Not knowing the work of his hands never had a chance to last.
Not knowing the work of his hands would soon be a thing of the past.

My brother finally began the work intended for him; his enduring task.
Not knowing destinies could be covered up by successes' mask;
Not knowing destinies' objects would soon lay him in a casque.

My own soul ran in place at every pit stop I found;
Not knowing I was trying to live in a campground.
Not knowing I was trying to ignore wisdom's sound.

When nothing appeals to your famished appetite,
And even hunger begins to lose its barking might.
When nothing appeals to your insatiable desires,
And unfulfilled dreams make us out to be liars.
When nothing appeals to your parched tongue,
And your seat at the wedding feast outward has swung.
When nothing appeals to your need to adventure,
And unknown human heart regions become your treasure.
When nothing appeals to your need to know and be known,
And you begin the journey every human makes alone.
When nothing appeals to your need to love and be loved,
And you learn that your every loose word spoken is observed.

Way, Truth, Life

He is the way to escape your haunting past.
He is the truth that God's love for you will last.
He is the life eternal found by the downcast.

Destiny, Fate

It's not what you're born into or what you're given;
Life is not a poker game of fated winners and losers.
It's what you do with what you've got while liv'in;
Life is a preliminary trial sifting stewards from abusers.

Perfect Will

Doing the right thing for the right reasons;
Like planting and reaping in nature's seasons.
Doing the right thing for the wrong reasons;
Like good intentioned puppet stings for demons.

The Irony of Faith

Nothing kills faith faster than a miracle;
Ironic how faith grows in the skeptical.
Nothing kills hope faster than choosing to ignore its ache;
Ironic how hope grows in those who treasure it though it break.
Nothing kills love faster than getting your felt needs met;
Ironic how love grows in affection's absence while repaying redemption's dept.

I am the Problem

The fool looks at the world's tragedy and; in ignorance, accuses his maker.
All causes of injustice; from a mirror, accuse the wise to be a selfish caretaker.
The wise man endures tragedy; knowing he shares the blame.
All that infects humanity cultivated within fools who judge the same.

Know Thyself

The degree that you know yourself is the degree you will know others.
Though every heart's well has a bottom, few draw beneath callousness.
The depth of your relations predetermined by self-denial that smothers.
Though deep calls to deep; shallowness is sure to beget shallowness.

Faith

Faith is holding tightly to a fading memory of an echo of his whisper.
Acting as if his word inevitable; though we recount worse than a lisper.

Politics and Religion

Many can attest the bridges burnt by discoursing religion and politics;
Yet what other hope is there to set about bridging such opposing sides?
Many more deny the affairs of an eternal kingdom centered on a crucifix;
Yet where else are righteous religion and politics harmonized in him that abides?

The more polarized the position the sooner one isolates into a party of one;
Yet the greater the influence in those who mitigate betwixt such patriotism.
The more watered down a conviction the larger a company of fools will have begun;
Yet the less likely to achieve its ideal just as it is with imposing fascism.

Control

Control is an illusion; there are only two masters, and you are not one of them.
Mankind reserves the right to choose their master; sinful nature, or Jesse's stem.

Tragic Falling Short

The greatest tragedy in creation occurs daily in heaven;
Sons and daughters feasting without noticing their lord's absence,
The greatest miracle in creation occurs daily for saints earthen;
Sons and daughters basking in his face without a shred of cognizance.

Sources of Identity

If you let others tell you who you are you'll act out their script.
If you tell yourself who you are your own destiny you'll restrict.
If you let the lord tell you who you are a unique fate he'll predict.

Confidence vs. Arrogance vs. Insecurity

Confidence is perceived as arrogance to the insecure or incompetent.
Arrogance is coveted by the insecure but loathed by the confident.
Insecurity is noticed by the confident but abused by the arrogant.

Awareness + Ability = Responsibility

Being aware of a problem you can do something about makes you responsible.
Being ignorant of righteous ways does not mean you cease to be accountable.
The good you know or have now; do not withhold from your neighbor.
The ill you have been spared will fall on your head if instead, you belabor.

"Recovery"

If your recovery never ends, it's a crutch;
Like a man who uses a cane for fashion soon begins limping.
If your growth never ends, its by heaven's touch;
Like a man benefits himself choosing generosity over skimping.

Every Virtue is a Verb

Only a religious man can be satisfied with actionless words.
Only a faithless man is satisfied with actions alone.
Every corrupt man settles for a place among pleasure's herds.
Every faithful man lives unpredictably; by the spirit blown.

Humility?

Humility is a figment of man's narrow-minded imagination;
Masking varying degrees of ignorance to intended station.
Exalting oneself like the youth that clambers atop the pile in a gas chamber;
Lowering oneself like the elder that only achieves
forgiveness when he can't remember.

Habits vs. Plans

Habits are for today, plans are for tomorrow.
Planning today taints the seeds we were to sough.
Living for tomorrow is sure to bear anxiety; turning hair gray.
The habits of tomorrow are either broken or reinforced today
Living in the moment is sure to bear fruit if we remember to pray.
Planning tomorrow's duties like awaiting the sun though it set low.
Habits are double edged swords; cutting many a friend and foe.

Graduation

Graduation, graduation...
How I wish I could fill you with emulation, But the fact of the matter is this;
You will soon realize that obliviousness really is bliss.
God is throwing you into the unknown;
Though in your own eyes you're not yet fully grown.
Never pass up a chance to learn;
Devotion offers that for which people yearn.

So anyways...
I've tried to teach you to see through the haze;
Many ears that hear my words are cursed,
And if you succeed; and heed, you'll be a first.
Not too long from now,
Brokenhearted and wondering how,
How you allowed yourself to become
That which you despised before you were numb.

Like I said,
You've been amply fed.
Now enter the race;
To try and make the world a better place!

A Yoke That Is Easy and A Burden That Is Light

A Yoke that is Easy and a Burden that is Light;
An invitation to flickering flames lest they lose their light.

Where is the hardship that the skeptical see in your law?
Surely your compassion intends to spare us from strife's draining paw.

Where is the cruelty the hesitant see in Yahweh rearing his child?
Surely your mercy reaches your kids, be they obedient or wild.
Where is the hardship the slothful see in your burden and bit?
Surely you're a kind father who gives an identity and destiny that fit.
Where is the asceticism the willful see in your stipulated prohibitions?
Surely your hedonism includes all creation, provided a few conditions.
Where is the wrath that the timid fear in your firm rod and staff?
Surely your commitment to us entails favor and discipline; each a half.
Where is the shrewdness the narrow-minded see in your repaying in kind?
Surely your impartiality makes you a judge like no other we could ever find.

Surely you are just and know we would be better off by being fair in our dealings.
Where is the cruelty the jaded attribute to your adopting the lost and weaklings?
Surely you are holy and your holiness demands separation till you make us distinct.
Where is the fine line we straddle while both your ways and your people go extinct?
Surely you are faithful and just want us to be devoted to what is best for others.
Where is the exclusiveness the cynical see in your calling only the obedient brothers?
Surely you are truthful and prefer our yes to be yes and our no to be no.
Where are the contradictions the picky get hung by in your advancing status quo?

Surely you are pure and made us to be distinct rather
than conform to a perceived norm.
Where is the arbitrariness faultfinders manufacture from your concealing your form?

Surely you are true and just want us to be truthful in all things, be they big or small.
Surely you are loving and just want us to be loving to friend and strangers all.
Surely you are forgiving and just want us to forget the wrongs done to us we accrue.
Surely you are pure and appreciate the distinctness
that makes us unique AND like you.

God is a Selective Genie

God is a selective genie,
So be careful what you wish for.
He daily probes what our heart's desire will be,
And re-arranges creation to settle love's score.

Will you; in faith, desire the unknown and unseen,
And be tempted by God's kingdom vision foreseen?
Or will you desire what you see of your neighbors,
And be tempted by the short-lived fruit of their labors?

The wisdom you thought you needed to govern may become a heavy burden.
The matrimony you wanted may become a bit that won't let you get a word in.
The glory of war may become just more baggage you can't tell.
The dream you have long sought may turn you into a hollow shell.

The apple of your eye may become the thorn in your side.
The joy of embarking may become the reason you fail to abide.

The uniqueness you sought may become your pitfall of pride.
The pleasure yearned for may turn your life into a boring ride.

Desiring that his will be done through his body in this place,
Ensures a prize awaits you at the end of this rugged race.
Desiring that his kingdom be manifest in our midst,
Ensures that the comforter provide all that we have missed.

The Virtue of Emptiness

By occupying our physical senses we stifle the spiritual,
Though humans are made of both the atrophy of either is gradual.
Anxious activity clutters the capacity of heart, mind, and soul,
By emptying ourselves we become available to play the son of man's role.

There once was a young man who came calling after an ancient teacher;
A budding adult seeking truth and enlightenment that it might go well with him.
The teacher served a cup of tea then kept pouring till it spilled all over,
"There's little room for new life when your cup is already filled to the brim."

We are the teacups filled to the brim with stale backwater,
While the son of man's teachings pour in then flow over.

We are the saturated sponges covered in stains and mold,
While all creation gushes with the nature of its master's household.

We are the packs filled with what we deem the daily necessities,
While the pilgrim's path contorts to steal our idols and rarities.

An empty belly spreads a table for divine delicacies,
Delicacies of loving kindness that are sure to nourish for centuries.
Neglected flesh prepares the heart for a heavenly embrace,
An embrace of grace that leaves no trace of disgrace.
Still and silent rooms set the stage for God to speak,
Speak strength and courage to the weary and weak.
A plugged nose clears the olfactory for eternity's scent,
Scent pleasing to the lord as we bear hearts with praise or lament.
An inward gaze opens the eyes to spy upon eternity's shores,
Shores that reflect events of past, present, and future heart-wars.

An occupied ear will either be deaf to truth or be unable to discern its source.
Be still and you will hear the rumble of God's kingdom expeditionary force.

An occupied heart will either be numb to love or unable to reciprocate.
Be still and you will be available to the heart of God's word incarnate.

An occupied spirit will either miss or covet the movement of the holy spirit,
Be still and you will soon discern the comforter's flow that only heirs inherit.

Occupied eyes will never see beyond your worldview of opinion.
Be still and you will be entrusted with the secrets of God's kingdom.

An occupied schedule leaves little time to entertain angels or the lord,
Be still and you will reserve time for pauper and king in the same temporal chord.

If you yearn to embark on an adventure so grand it seems an allegory,
Be still until Jesus' commission becomes your new and better reality.

If you desire to taste of eternal pleasure that shivers through flesh and spirit,
Be still until the suffering servant standard no longer threatens to inhibit.

If you would aspire to gaze upon the horizon of heaven's divide,
Be still and know revelation comes when you let your agendas subside.

Emptiness is the virtue-less virtue that paves the way for all divine qualities;
Emptiness is the canvas reserved for the lord to paint whatever he please.

Better one handful with peace and tranquility than toil and strife;
Better still, two empty hands tied by a cross to grasp eternal life.

Perpetual Dry Mouth

Love, faith, and hope are the only ways to fill a heart to the brim,
While death, disease and darkness will make any light grow dim,

A drop of faith from a discerning official that doesn't bother check'in,
Or from seasonal fall that spreads its seeds though winter beckon,

A splash of hope from a child who believes he can become anything he wants,
Or from childhood memories of outdoor summer revelry that still haunts,

A gulp of love from a vulnerable heart lowering its veil,
Or from an endless quest for the miracle of the holy grail,

A drop of beauty from the heart of a youth's budding romance,
Or from fleeting clouds flirting lazily across Heaven's expanse,

A drop of wisdom from a reminiscing elder,
Or from the diligent ant to which the wise defer,

A splash of grace from a friend bearing a burden not his own,
Or from a ripe fruit tree that sprang not from seed you had sown,

He who drains others dry ensures his own fate to progressively die,
He who refreshes others with grace and mercy ensures his own seat on high,

The real question at the end of the day,
Is whether I fill your cup with what I do and say,
Or if I'm so dry I sap your well no matter how brief my stay.

Principles of Influence

Reciprocation is the 'give and take' that both begins
and sustains most human relations;
It's like the gears on a dial that are sure to turn back toward their starting positions.

Indebtedness is the heart-debt that must be repaid when accepting any help or favor;
It's like a thief's welcoming embrace that is sure to leave behind a bittersweet flavor.

Reject-then-retreat traps others by falling into a pit so as to be lent a helping hand;
It's like manufacturing guilt then offering relief in
the form of a favor already planned.

Consistency is the grooves for our will that are made
by each attitude and action forevermore;
It's like the formation of a tel foundation that repeatedly
leaves stubborn walls taller than before.

A fixed-action-pattern is our automatic matching of
similar behavior to similar situations;
It's like birds seeking morning worms though mother
nature never conforms to stipulations.

A foot-in-the-door request bypasses unconscious barriers
and plants a 'yes' on our lips that'll stick;
It's like a student asking if they can go to see the nurse
then soon after asking to go home sick.

The Universal Testimony

I once was deaf; ever hearing but never understanding,
But now I hear life's whisper gently guiding yet never commanding.
I once was blind; ever seeing but never perceiving,
But now all mysteries are laid bare by simply believing.

I once was mute; ever speaking but never knowing my own voice,
But now living water spills out from every loving word and choice.
I once was numb; ever tasting but never knowing pleasure's touch,
But now joy and pleasure mark every step I take within his clutch.

I once was a slave; scratching myself raw with every sinful itch,
But now freedom permits all things so long as I question if they tarnish or enrich.
I once was dead; a whitewashed tomb scrambling to mask the stench of decay,
But now eternal life builds up his home in me every time I serve or pray.

I once was alone; left to fend for myself like a youth without wisdom's guiding word,
But now a great cloud of witnesses supports my every step toward the good shepherd.
I once was stunted; a heart and mind that plateaued long before their prime,
But now blessings and tragedies leave my heart bigger each and every time.

Yeah, But...

When friends and family say my naive purity is immature,
I'll say, "Yeah, but ignorance is the price to keep my heart pure."

When my brother guides me toward pleasure's tainted well,
I'll say, "Yeah, but only he who created my thirst can (it) quell."

When my stomach grumbles that my father's table does not satiate,
I'll say, "Yeah, but my daily bread is far more than the meal I ate."

When an appealing voice implies that riches ought to litter the path heavenward,
I'll say, "Yeah, but my big brother walked my wretched
route before he could be my lord."

When a serpent's whisper draws my attention to an easy path,
I'll say, "Yeah, but the route to hell is known by its rotten aftermath."

When any heavenly being speaks ill of the mighty author of my feeble faith,
I'll say, "Yeah, but I have found freedom and life in every word he say'ith."

When any demonic oppressor gloats over my fragile flesh or spirit,
I'll say, "Yeah, but the name of Jesus is solid ground that will never quit."

When you accurately accuse me to my face with my faults of yesterday,
I'll say, "Yeah, but Jesus' blood paved over my ruts of sin with a better way."

When Jesus himself says it's not fitting to offer the heirs' portion to their pets,
I'll say, "Yeah, but I'm satisfied by even the crumbs from the table your father sets."

When Satan suggests that God has withheld any good thing,
I'll say, "Yeah, but true freedom only comes when to the cross I cling."

When the world shakes a hostile fist at me for having a closed mind,
I'll say, "Yeah, but narrow is the path to life and wide
the route that hellward does wind."

When any priest or shepherd labels me a whitewashed tomb,
I'll say, "Yeah, but even death's scent can't keep me from my groom."

When a haunting memory drags yesterday's shame to the forefront of my mind,
I'll say, "Yeah, but when my father forgives not even a trace of shame will you find."

When heaven's prosecution claims my obedience is only as deep as his blessing,
I'll say, "Yeah, but even if my tongue is taken from
me his praise I'll still be expressing."

When a lying tongue speaks the truth that my life's seeds fall in dry and rocky places,
I'll say, "Yeah, but the offering of my life is for my lover and not for other's graces."

When common sense suggests my fruitless labor of love is a waste of time,
I'll say, "Yeah, but within my life an ageless branch grows that's always in its prime."

When a liberal attitude bombards my culture saying
our bodies are ours to do with as we see fit,
I'll say, "Yeah, but this clay jar gladly accepts the
liberation that comes with the spirit's bit."

When a gruesome wretch speaks from experience
that god's love is not unconditional,
I'll say, "Yeah, but any cost was overpaid by his son on a cross as our supplemental."

Discipleship 101

By definition discipleship is to be a learner in another's way.
Discipleship turns us into a dispenser of another's truth.
Discipleship grafts us into another's will, thoughts, and life.

Learners of history so that we don't repeat the mistakes of the past.
Learners of His story so that we navigate the narrow path steadfast.
Learners of love so that the world be proven cold and heartless by contrast.
Learners of faith so that we are undeterred by snares that leave many aghast.
Learners of hope so we receive heirship though an outcast.
Learners of justice so that the creator's image be
seen and honored among the downcast.
Learners of wisdom so that men might avoid polarized
extremes that fuel every newscast.

Unlike any other craft, there will never be a path to mastery;
Only hands and feet that learn to defer to their teacher in a hurry.

Unlike any other revolution, progress is not measured by success;
Only seeds that fall to the earth that multiply by becoming less.

Unlike any other good intentioned agenda, charisma is detrimental;
Only prodigals learn to bring others in without being judgmental.

Discipleship is the surgeon's blade that removes cancerous tumors;
The winnowing fork used to sift out the chaff that came to hear rumors.

Discipleship is the direction-less road map home with vague traveling advice;
The haunting voice calling us to set out for foreign lands no matter the price.

Discipleship is the limitless bar that gets raised as we labor and train;
The thinning of the flock that would balk at going against the grain.

Discipleship is the food for the son of man that men know nothing of;
The fruitful evidence that the spirit rests on the son of man like a dove.

Jesus' discipleship lets sinners cut their piece of the cake and also eat it.
Our discipleship like forcing laws and regulations down another's throat.
Jesus' discipleship is a yoke that is easy and a bit that is sure to fit.
Our discipleship like inviting the drowning onto our own sinking boat.

Discipleship is the unending introduction into heavenly affairs;
The fork in the road that either ascends or descends to dark lairs.

Discipleship is the daily death to self that leaves the heart bigger than before;
The rough stone that either sharpens or shatters each heart that seeks his door.

We often say you can only lead others as far as you have gone,
But the path to maturity is a custom route laid out like a marathon.

We often say that bad company corrupts good morals,
But the path to influence begins with dirtied sandals.

We often say that each man is the sum of his experiences,
But the path to fruitfulness has little to do with our advances.

We often say that if you don't have anything nice to say remain silent,
But the path to life begins with sharp words and a heart willing to repent.

The Jewel of Creation

As it is when glimpsing the lord; gleaning the son of
God akin to missing the son of man,
But do not assume you have seen all there is to see of him, or of his audacious plan.

As it is when inspecting a diamond; glimmers of you will be seen,
But do not assume you have anything in common with its sheen.

As it is when peering out a foggy window; the closer you get the more you fog it up,
But do not assume your perspective will improve as you become more of a grown-up.

As it is when using a microscope to inspect a person's
cells; you may find the same building blocks,
But do not assume your door-to-door salesmanship resembles
the one who from heart-to-heart knocks.

As it is when gazing into a kaleidoscope; he plays different tricks on every set of eyes,
But do not assume the substance of truth changes
with every seeker; that, to Jesus cries.

As it is when inspecting a home's foundation; what is
on the surface is sure to warrant concern,
But do not assume if your savior stood before you that
his identity you could (at once) discern.

Looking for the lion we are sure to find the lamb;
Lamb worth more than the world's every ram.
Looking for the lamb we are sure to find the lion;
Lion of Judah leading the van as heaven's scion.

Looking for the judge we are sure to find he's delegated our brother;
Brother we rejected because he claimed the lineage of another.
Looking for our brother we are sure to find he's our judge;
Judge that imposes his father's will and refuses to budge.

Looking for the great physician we are sure to find he prefers teaching;
Teaching children that his father's house is not beyond their reaching.
Looking for the good teacher we are sure to find the great physician;
Physician ready to operate before describing our deadly condition.

Looking for the yoke that is easy we are sure to find his heavy heart;
Heavy heart bearing the weight of our offense that would tear us apart.
Looking for his heavyhearted wisdom we are sure to find his easy yoke;
Yoke that is so easy we may; at some point, suspect that it may have broke.

Looking for the reigning lord we are sure to find the suffering servant;
Servant who suffered in Gethsemane, but to his father's plan bent.
Looking for the servant familiar with suffering we are sure to find the reigning lord;
Lord who imposes his will onto all creation till Heaven and Earth be of one accord.

Looking for the revolutionary we are sure to find a pillar of establishment;
Establishment of an upside-down kingdom sustained among impoverishment.
Looking for the pillar of establishment we are sure
to find the Nazarene revolutionary;
Revolutionary that liberates: Heaven, Earth, then
Hell by following the spirit's itinerary.

Looking for the revealed truth we are sure to find he is often concealed;
Concealed even from the crowds and disciples that saw cripples healed.
Looking for the concealed truth we are sure to find his truth revealed among youth;
Youth that are sure to receive his blessing though
they; in many ways, remain uncouth.

Potency and Proximity

Potency is the degree others are impacted by experiencing who you are.
Proximity is how near you draw (by default) to both strangers and friends.
Dullness is what you get if you let the heart and mind daily lower the bar.
Distance is a measuring stick keeping others away that breaks before it bends.

Potency with proximity is like food coloring that is sure to dye any liquid.
Potency without proximity is like a snack on a shelf that's out of reach.
Dullness with distance like salted soil producing fruit uneatable and insipid.
Dullness without distance is like debris that will ruin every engine they breach.

Those who are potent needn't add more fuel to the campfire,
For strengthening your strength is like creating a lopsided pyre.
Those who are proximal needn't invite more to their campground,
For only the ones who can stay warm on cold nights will stick around.

What good is a bonfire that scatters sparks and burns?
And a heart full of envy than never learns?
What good is a saltshaker never at the table?
And a mind in the clouds that treats life as a fable?
What good is a light that is hidden under your bed?
And a peace that is snuffed before a drop of blood is shed?
What good is truth that never gets heard?
And a mouth that never speaks a word?
What good are colors that never touch the paper?
And a faith that daily dissipates like morning due to vapor?

Over-familiarity

Surely familiarity breeds boredom, and boredom breeds stagnation.
Stagnation of the heart warping the nature of God's favored creation.
Surely mystery breeds intrigue, and intrigue breeds experiential exploration.
Exploration of the heart that fashioned a world to be our formative station.

Stagnation proportional to familiarity;
The more thorough the familiarity the less emotion will accompany.
Growth proportional to mystery;
The more thorough the mystery the less a spectator in God's story.

Familiarity comforts with one hand but maims with the other.
The other reinforcing fruitless cycles that suffocate and smother.
Mystery entrances at first glance but terrifies if it remains.
It remains in/for the son of man marked by Jesus' blood stains.

Over-familiarity with people will cause you to see and use them as objects.
Over-familiarity with sights traps you in a maze alongside ignorant subjects.
Over-familiarity with sounds severs the ear that hears from the heart that inspects.
Over-familiarity with sensations degrades pleasures to an itch that scratching infects.
Over-familiarity with routines like preferring slavery
over freedom daunting and complex.
Over-familiarity with hobbies subtly laces play with toil and rest with works.

Knowing what a man will do and become causes time with them will depreciate.
Knowing how a story will end makes every twist of
plot seem like a rigid and cruel fate.
Knowing what is around the corner ensures you'll
never notice anything new or great.
Knowing where life will take you like being stuck in a game of unending checkmate.

Knowing which relations endure would cause you
to cut ties left and right and alienate.
Knowing the path ahead is as freeing as it is restricting of our perpetually clean slate.

Lack familiarity and your roots won't get their needed nutrients.
Lack spontaneity and your fruit will surely rot before it even ripens.
Preserving mystery like harvesting (in season) life's sweetest ingredients.
Preserving stagnation like re-watching a horror flick that no longer frightens.

Just like an old timer's life can amount to daily reminiscing over coffee,
But an elder who bridges generational gaps becomes a sheltering tree.
Just like a year-round summer dulls its warmth on your skin,
But tasting winter's chill enhances summer's tanning sensation.
Just like running a closed circuit encourages situational obliviousness,
But finding your way off track can drown you in freedom's vastness.

Seasonality of Friendship

The ages have affirmed that there is a season for every activity.
Although each coin has two sides, a spectator loses objectivity.
There are as many kinds of friends as there are seasons in life.
Although none can be replaced, why weather needless strife?
The wise man knows he must first inspect and hone his own will.
May wisdom guide her children so that our destiny we can fulfill.

There are friends that will treat you like family or the closest of kin,
but thousands more always think of nothing but their own skin.
There are friends that will always want what is best for you,
but thousands more hide their selfishness with promises untrue.
Surely there are friends for every season under the sun.
Perhaps their variety is what keeps a reckless life fun.

Some only stick around as long as your pockets are full,
Others are sure to return tenfold every generous handful.
Some only show up to share a drink when winter drags on,
Others are sure to welcome you no matter how early the dawn.

As for me, what kind of friend was I yesterday?
Can I see a path of sprouting seeds following my way?
As for me, what kind of friend am I today?
Do I do the deeds and say the words only I can say?
As for me, what kind of friend will I be tomorrow?
Will my heart grow bigger or will it shrink from constant sorrow?

If I am naive how can I speak of life with authority?
But if corrupt, how to avoid snaring myself in duplicity?
If I am selfless how can I keep my own cup full?
But if selfish, how can I refrain from words that are cruel?

If I am heartless how can my words of comfort have meaning?
But if I care too much, how can I avoid incessantly intervening?
If I am always productive and busy working, how can I share my time?
But if I am always available, how can I devote myself to reach my prime?
If my head is in the clouds how can I draw near to your heart?
But if I am down to Earth, how to see the big picture and be set apart?
If I am possessive how can I be glad when others make you shine and grow?
But if entrust to fate, how to seize the moment and let my heart of hearts show?

Even a stranger can comfort for a night out of pity,
But a friend won't hesitate to get their own hands dirty.
Even a vagabond can get you believing your charity is grand,
But a friend won't rely on flattery when asking for a helping hand.
Even a cruel manager can deal respectfully out of responsibility,
But a friend will bring a smile to your face even with stupidity.

An Empty Tomb

There has only been one subject Jesus warned me to avoid teaching,
Who am I to speak of Gethsemane's cup he never stopped drinking?
There was only one tree in the garden Adam was warned to avoid eating,
Who are we to aspire to equality with the creator we are daily meeting?

Who am I but another Peter willing to deny my Lord if my accusers desist?
There was only one rabbi raising the moral bar even while he hung by the wrist.
Who are we to fathom the offense of mockers that strikes even deeper than their fist?
There has only been one man whose blood was
powerful enough to leave sin dismissed.

There was only one man who entered hell's gates as
a convict and walked out victorious.
Who am I but another friend missing your wedding
feast while you invite the inglorious?
There has only been one to shed clothes of omniscience to dine with the notorious.
Who are we to root for you from sidelines and not
join in your Father's work laborious?

Who am I to skip over the three'ish days you labored
by Hades' lake the same as Galilee?
There was only one man who could have turned hell
into heaven if he had stayed past three.
Who are we to point others to the tomb when it's
often our hearts that are left empty?
There has only been one God who backs up his promise
to send his spirit to make his home in me.

The scary truth for all to see
is that a cross and tomb are the center of eternity.
The profound truth that a lamb's slaughter outlast
every deed of present, future, and past.
The scary truth that every buffer zone
between God and man replaced by an invading throne.
The profound truth that all can receive
the power of the God-man Jesus if they just believe.